The Mum's Guide to Returning to Work –

A Step By Step Guide to Finding a Job After Having Children

BEKKI CLARK

To Martin, Molly and Grace – thank you.

To the many women I have worked with over the last few years. Thank you for your inspiration. This book is for you.

Copyright © Bekki Clark
First published in 2010 by:
Beamington Publishing

The right of Bekki Clark to be identified as the author of this work has been asserted by her in accordance with the copyright, Designs and Patents Act 1988.

ISBN 978-1-4457-6103-9

The Mum's Guide to Returning to Work

Contents

The Mum's Guide to Returning to Work

Acknowledgements

I couldn't have written this book without the many clients I have worked with over the past eight years at Cambridge Women's Resources Centre. You have inspired, challenged and encouraged me. To the women who have been on my 'Return to Work' courses, thank you for the chance to try out my ideas and materials on you.

To my colleagues past and present at CWRC, I have learnt so much from you and appreciate your support in this project. In particular thank you to Christine, Pauline, Pat and Lesley who have taught me so much. I'm sure many of the ideas in this book were yours originally and I'm sorry if I've stolen them from you!

I am also grateful to all the women who told me their stories and let me use their quotes and case studies at various points in the book.

Thank you to Celia Phipps, Martin Clark, Kate Blackwell, Alice Thornton and Julie Gabriel for their thorough proof-reading and constructive comments on the many drafts of the book.

To Martin, who encouraged me to start the book, helped me to find the time to write it and supported me in keeping going when I felt like giving up, thank you. To Molly and Grace, I don't know how many times you've said: 'Mummy, are you still writing that book?', I'm sorry for spending so long on this!

Finally to the beautiful women – friends, colleagues and clients - who let me take their photos for the front cover, thank you all.

Bekki Clark
September 2010

Chapter One

Introduction - Setting the Scene

Finding work is not an easy process at the best of times, but throw into the mix five years' experience of changing nappies, sleepless nights and dealing with toddler tantrums and it puts the whole process into a different light.

Nothing is straightforward any more. You are a different person, with different priorities. You have gained new skills and are feeling rusty with other ones. Your confidence is at an all time low, you don't know what job you could possibly do that fits in with your family and you haven't got the first clue how (or even whether) to describe your 'career break' on your CV.

> According to career development website A Brave New World: *'It is almost impossible to put a clear figure on how many people are out there thinking about getting back to work, but we know that it's a very large pool of women and it's an important target group because of the demographics that are being faced by companies in the future, older and ageing population, older workers and fewer younger people to fill the gaps in the marketplace etc.* [1]

Being a full-time mum can be both hugely rewarding and totally exhausting. Unfortunately it is an undervalued role in today's society. For many mums, the prospect of finding a job can be daunting, but this book sets out to support you on the journey.

Who is this book for?

This book is primarily aimed at women who have had a break from work to bring up their children and are now looking to return, commonly known as 'women returners'. It is not specifically for women on maternity leave who have a job to return to, or for women who have had a break from work for other reasons, such as ill health or caring for an elderly relative; however, they may well find many aspects of it useful.

You may have been at home with your child(ren) for one, five, ten or even twenty years. You may have been at home out of choice or because you couldn't afford the costs of childcare, or perhaps you couldn't find a suitable job when your children were young. You may be married, living with your partner or be a lone parent. You could be in your 20s, 30s, 40s or even 50s. During this time you may have done some studying, voluntary work, a 'fill-in' part-time job, or none of the above. Now, you are ready to kick-start your career again, either returning to a field you are experienced in, or to something new.

There are a growing band of dads who are taking primary responsibility for bringing up their children and when they choose to return to work, they will be facing many of the same issues as any woman returner. I hope that they too will find this book useful. However, I hope you will forgive me for pandering to the majority and making the assumption throughout that the reader is a woman and a mother. If this doesn't apply to you I apologise!

Facts:
3.4 million women with dependent children are not currently working[2]
1 million women want to work but feel they cannot[3]
830,000 lone parents are not in paid work[4]

What are the issues?

The issues for women returning to work are huge. You may feel anxious and bewildered about the journey ahead, not sure what skills you have and what kind of job you could do. You may lack confidence in your ability to work, having been out of the market for so long. You may have no idea how to go about writing a CV, or how to prepare for an interview. You may be wondering how to find a part-time job that will fit in, as far as possible, with your children's school hours. Perhaps you are a lone parent or from overseas and are now feeling that you don't know where to start looking for a job; it just seems too difficult.

About the book

This book is intended to help you deal with all these issues, in the hope that you will, when you are ready, find a job that is rewarding and gives you a work-life balance that suits your needs. It offers no guarantees, but I hope it will give you the encouragement and support you need to give it a go. This book is not about telling 'stay-at-home' mums that they should be going out to work, but offering support to those that have decided that they need or want to.

Each chapter is written with the woman returner in mind, dealing with questions relevant to their situation, such as: 'who can I use as a referee?' or 'what skills have I developed whilst being at home with children?' It provides invaluable tips and suggestions as well as quotes and case studies from women in similar situations. It aims to be practical, uplifting and easy to read.

A career is often compared with going on a journey. The first part of this book aims to help you work out where you are starting from and where you are trying to get to in your career journey. Chapter Two looks at how you can make the most of your time at home with children, to prepare you for an eventual return to work. Chapter Three addresses the crucial issue of confidence, without which a return to work will be an uphill struggle. Chapter Four helps you to identify what type of work may be appropriate for you and Chapter Five looks at opportunities to work for yourself.

The second part of the book aims to help you to work out how to get there: Chapters Six, Seven, Eight and Nine will help you to identify where to look for job vacancies, how to apply for jobs and succeed at interview; while Chapters Ten, Eleven and Twelve look at how to make a job work for you, addressing flexible working, childcare and finances in turn. Managing the transition back to the world of work is a challenge for many women, so Chapters Thirteen and Fourteen cover assertiveness and time management. Finally Chapters Sixteen and Seventeen are specifically aimed at women from overseas and lone parents, addressing some of the particular issues which they will encounter on their journey.

What is my story?

A careers adviser, trainer and coach, I work for the charity Cambridge Women's Resources Centre providing one-to-one support and training courses to women who want to return to the workplace. Not only do I work with women returners, but I've been one too. I have two daughters and stopped working when my second child was born, returning a couple of years later when I finally found a job that suited me. I work with women from all walks of life and love seeing women gain in confidence as they start to believe that they can work again. Many of them have now happily settled back into the workplace and I know that you can too.

Chapter Two

Where are you now?

Why do you want to return to work?

Many of you will be reading this because you have got to a stage in your family life when you are ready (or perhaps even desperate) to return to work. For others, it may not be a choice. Perhaps your family finances are such that you can't afford not to work, maybe relationship breakdown has forced the issue, or as a lone parent the Jobcentre is telling you that now your youngest child has reached a certain age, you will no longer be able to claim income support.

Before setting out on your journey back to the workplace, take some time to think about why you want to start working again. Reflecting on your motivation will help you to consider what kind of job to do, how many hours to do, or indeed whether now is the right time for you to work. The following are some of the reasons women have given me for returning to work:

- Getting out of the house.
- Financial necessity.
- Financial independence.
- Improving status.
- Escaping boredom.
- Developing a career.
- Embarking on a career before it is too late.
- Pressure from the Jobcentre.
- Wanting to develop/use skills and talents.
- Meeting people.
- Getting over a bereavement or separation.
- Improving self-image.
- Setting an example for the children.
- Using your brain.
- Escaping the mess in the kitchen/on the floor/everywhere.
- Needing to prove something to someone.
- Children have started school.
- Seeking new interests.
- Re-establishing a sense of identity, not just someone's mother or partner.
- The children are old enough now.

- A sense of achievement.
- Children have left home.
- To prove you are still young enough to do it.
- Gaining more qualifications.

Indeed you may have many other reasons. None of these are necessarily good or bad reasons to return to work, but it may be useful to consider what your reasons are.

When is the right time to return?

There is no right or wrong time to go back to work, you need to consider what is right for you and your family. Much of the decision will be based on your answers to why you want to restart your career and how important those reasons are to you. Do you want to get back to work fairly quickly before you start to feel de-skilled? Or do you want to make the most of having pre-school children at home? How do you feel about your children going to part-time or full-time childcare, or going to after school and holiday clubs?

Some women will have a short break of a year or two, whilst their children are still very young. Others go back to work when their youngest has settled into primary, or even secondary school, I know some women who haven't wanted to go back to work until their youngest child has left home, after a break of maybe twenty years! Interestingly a trigger for some women stopping work has been their children starting primary or secondary school. Presumably this is due to the logistics of childcare becoming more complicated at this stage, or maybe they feel that their children's needs have changed.

If you're not yet ready to return to work, what's holding you back? The safe option might be to stay at home, but is this really the right option for you and your family? It may well be, but perhaps it is just inertia keeping you where you are; the routine you have now is familiar and big changes can be unsettling. Or maybe a fear of failure or the unknown is stopping you from making a move back into the world of work? If it is a lack of confidence that is stopping you, you might like to move on to Chapter Three to look at how to build your confidence. Have a think through what the benefits of being back at work might be for you. How would it make you feel? Positive? Satisfied? Financially better off? Or just plain stressed?

How many hours do you want to work?

Do you want to work full-time or part-time? The opportunities for working part-time are increasing, but employers still have a long way to go. Part-time work, when it can be found can be an excellent compromise for someone who wants a career and to spend time with their children. However, does it have to be you working part-time? If you have a partner and you believe that your family would function better with only one adult working full-time, perhaps you could encourage your partner to look at working more flexible hours. Chapter Ten will look at flexible working options in more detail.

How can I prepare for the future whilst I am still at home?

If you are not ready to go back to work just yet, you may like to consider how to make the most of your time at home, to make the step back to work that bit easier when you are ready. We all know that looking after young (particularly pre-school) children can be an exhausting, all consuming and a full-time job. You may have no time to think about making your CV look good. However perhaps there are some things you could be doing that would fit in around your children. Anything you can do now, to learn new skills, keep up to date with old skills and to keep active will be useful in the future. Here are some suggestions:

- Voluntary work; this can be an excellent way of developing your skills, gaining some valuable work experience as well as giving you someone to give you an up to date reference. However, this may only be possible if you have some childcare available or your children are at school. If you do have time though, consider contacting your local volunteer centre about volunteering opportunities you could be involved in for just a few hours a week. It may be more practical to look at volunteering that you could do with your children; for example helping out with the local toy library or parent and toddler groups, helping to organise a school fair, or joining the fundraising committee for the local playgroup.

- Other things you could consider which show initiative and a variety of skills could include setting up a babysitting circle, supporting a campaign on a local issue such as getting the council to put a crossing on a busy junction, writing an article for a local parenting magazine or offering your skills to be a trustee for a local charity.

- Read when you get the chance. Reading novels for pleasure helps to keep your brain active, even better if you join a book group. Read newspapers to keep abreast of current affairs and policy development in your line of work. Take out a subscription to a journal relevant to your career area, to keep updated.

- Some employers, such as the civil service, offer 'keeping in touch' days for staff that are on maternity leave or a career break. This can help you to keep up to date with changes in your workplace, meet staff and learn about new technology etc. It may also be a good chance to network regarding new job opportunities which might arise.

- Learn some new skills or develop old ones by going on a course. Some colleges of further education or community education courses provide a crèche to enable women with pre-school children to study; or go to an evening class, if your partner can look after the children. You may want to study something of interest for pleasure, or something that may help your career progression. If your computer skills are self taught, this may be a good time to do an IT course so that you have evidence to show an employer that your skills are up to standard. If you can't get out to a course, consider doing a distance learning course from home.

The Mum's Guide to Returning to Work

- You may never have a better opportunity to retrain for a new career. You may not be ready to return to work, but you might want to consider studying full or part-time. It can sometimes be easier to fit studying around childcare needs than it is to fit work, but the costs of both childcare and tuition whilst not earning may well be a problem. Go to the end of this chapter for some suggestions as to websites which may help you in finding both courses and funding.

Most of the above activities can be used as evidence of skills that you possess. Most employers value and recognise skills and experiences developed through voluntary work, as well as through paid work. Try to keep a list of the things you've been involved with and have achieved since you stopped working, so that it is at your fingertips when you are ready to apply for that perfect job when it comes up!

Enjoy being at home

I remember being at the checkout in the supermarket with both my two-year-old and my young baby when an older woman said to me: 'enjoy your children while they are young, it won't be the same when they start school'. Having had a sleepless night with the baby and then having had to endure numerous toddler tantrums not only to get to the supermarket, but to get round it, enjoying my children felt like quite a tall order at that moment. Looking back, there are many things about small children that I don't miss, and it was very hard work, but some of the things I do miss are:
- Watching a small child learn something new every day.
- Laughing at the funny things toddlers say, when they are

learning new words.

- Time to have a coffee with friends whilst the children played, when not much else would have been achieved at home otherwise.
- Enjoying simple, free pleasures such as walking to the park, picking up fallen leaves and feeding the ducks.
- Being able to play with play dough all morning, because there's nowhere else we really had to be.
- Being able to wear what I wanted every day and not thinking about whether I was smart enough for work.
- Not having to be out of the house by a certain time.

> 'Life is what happens to you while you are busy making other plans.'
>
> John Lennon

At the risk of sounding like the older woman in the supermarket, do try to enjoy whatever stage you are at, as the next one will only be different. Whether you've chosen to be at home for now, or feel you have no choice, be glad of the things you can do, without having to fit work around them. Children don't stay young forever and you will have years ahead to pick up your career in the future.

I had initially thought I'd hate being at home, but actually I loved it, and really enjoyed doing things other than being a physiotherapist – I got very involved in running NCT groups, church women's groups, and became a school governor. I also started doing some colour consultancy work, fitting it around school and playgroup hours. I would've found it very stressful if I'd not gone to lots of groups, and made friends in the same situation as myself, because entertaining small children is hard work, for me!

Bridget

The 'Mini-Career'

If you worked in a stressful, responsible, high level job before you had children, you may feel that it will be some time before you feel ready to go back to that fast paced, pressurised life, with a job that comes home with you at the end of the day. This may particularly be the case if you worked in a field that you feel doesn't lend itself to part-time working. A lot of women I know in this position have chosen to do what I call a 'mini-career' for a few years when their children are young, with a view to going back to their former career or even a different one at a later stage.

A 'mini-career' could take many forms, but it could be something you are doing fairly part-time, perhaps to fit in with school hours. Maybe you are not working at the level or receiving the kind of pay you were used to before having children, but you are happy with that because you are glad to be working and earning something, however little. Chapter Five has a number of ideas to explore that involve working from home, such as direct selling, childminding or freelance work.

In the example above, Bridget worked from home doing some colour consultancy work, before returning to physiotherapy when her children were older. A friend of mine sold greetings cards at parties and school fairs, before finding work in childcare. Another friend currently works as a part-time school secretary, because that suits her at the moment, but she fully intends to go back to office management when her children are older.

Unfortunately women's part-time work in the U.K. tends to be characterised by low paid and low skilled jobs. If you are happy doing that kind of work as a mini-career for a few years, then that is fine. However many women work in these kinds of fields because that is all they can find and they then find themselves trapped there much longer than they may want to. You may be reading this book because you have been doing a 'mini-career' for a few years and now want to move on, in which case I do hope it will help you. If this is your situation, do challenge yourself to move on and not to get stuck in a rut. Do ask for help if you need it.

Goal setting

The prospect of returning to work can feel like a huge mountain to climb, but break it down into small manageable steps and it won't feel half as daunting. When something feels scary or challenging, it is so easy to put it off until tomorrow. Before you know it 'tomorrow' has become next year, or even five years time and you've still taken no action. Setting yourself goals and targets can really help to organise your thoughts and set you on the road to putting your plans into action. So, if you want to be back at work in say, two years time, start setting some goals now. Here's how to do it:

- You may want your goals to be long or short-term, career related or personal, serious or light-hearted.
- Break each of your goals into a series of manageable steps.
- Make sure you set a time for when you want to achieve each of your goals.
- Ask people to help you achieve your goals if it will help.
- Share your goals with others, so that they can encourage you on the journey and celebrate your success.
- Review your goals at regular intervals to see how you are getting on. Are you achieving your goals? If not, why not?
- Reward yourself when you have achieved a goal, with for example, a glass of wine, a night out or a shopping trip.

Your goals will be personal, but they might look something like this:

Goal	Steps	When by?
Decide what job to do	Make an appointment with a careers adviser	End Jan
	Get a book from the library	Next week
	Start talking to three friends about it	End Jan
Update IT skills	Look at local college website	End Jan
	Visit college	End Feb
	Look at Learndirect website	End Feb
	Start course	April
Get some voluntary work experience	Visit volunteer centre	End May
	Start volunteering	September
Update CV	Get book from library	End April
	Start writing CV	End May
	Ask friends for comments	End June
Think about childcare	Find out what is available locally	End May
	Ask friends for recommendations	End May

The Mum's Guide to Returning to Work

	Visit at least three childcare providers	End June
	Put name down provisionally for childcare	End July
Start applying for jobs	Start looking in the paper and websites	End July
	Apply for at least two jobs as a test-run	End September
	Apply for at least three jobs per month, if appropriate	October onwards
	Ask friend to help with a mock interview	End October
Personal goals	Start a new leisure activity once a week	End September
	Get children to start helping with more jobs at home	End October
	Get fit; start some form of exercise twice a week	End August
Review progress	Hopefully have found a job	End December
	If not, make another appointment with careers adviser or chat to a friend for advice	End December
	Review goals and set some new ones	End December

'A journey of a thousand miles starts with a single step'
Lau-tzu (Chinese philosopher born 604 BC)

Points to ponder

- Be clear about why you want to go back to work.
- Is now the right time to return?
- Enjoy your time at home now.
- Use your time to improve your future CV.

- Consider a "mini-career".
- Plan for the future and set some goals.

Information

Volunteering	Local volunteer centres	www.volunteering.org.uk
	National volunteering website	www.do-it.org.uk
Studying	For help in finding a local course	nextstep.direct.gov.uk (Find a Course) or ring the freephone Nextstep Advice Line on 0800 100 900
	Higher education courses	www.ucas.ac.uk
Distance Learning	National Extension College for GCSEs and A' levels	www.nec.ac.uk
	Open University for degree courses	www.open.ac.uk
	Alison for free courses in IT and business	www.alison.com
	learndirect offers courses in IT, business, personal development and basic skills, free for some learners. Either online or in a local learndirect centre	www.learndirect.co.uk
Funding for courses:	Career Development loans	www.direct.gov.uk/cdl
	Funding for higher education	www.studentfinance.direct.gov.uk

Chapter Three

Confidence Building –
Make Sure You Are Ready

Why does confidence matter?

It may surprise you to start looking at confidence so early on in the book, but without confidence you won't feel able to take the action you need to get back into work. This is the building block you need, in order to believe that you can work again and that you can aim high.

So what does it mean to be confident? Think of someone you know who appears to be confident. The chances are they:

- Are comfortable in their body and happy with their appearance.
- Are not shy about talking to new people.
- Smile and accept compliments gracefully and give compliments easily.
- See the positive in life, rather than making constant negative comments and criticisms.
- Live a full and active life, making the most of opportunities that come their way.
- Aren't scared to try something new.
- Change things they don't like about the world or their community, rather than just moaning about it.
- Move forward in their life and are always looking for the next big challenge.

Self-confidence is about having enough belief in ourselves that it leads to action. A lack of self-confidence can be hugely debilitating and hold us back from trying anything new or moving forwards in our life.

'According to employers, women returning to work after a break perform well in their jobs. But employers also say that many women returners lack confidence and this stops them from doing as well as they could in the workplace.'

Haygroup 2006[1]

Parenthood: an undervalued job

There are many barriers to returning to work for a woman with young children at home: lack of flexible working options, finding good childcare, outdated skills; but the biggest one I believe is a lack of confidence. Time and again I've talked to women who just don't believe in themselves and aren't convinced that they have anything to offer an employer. It becomes easy to make excuses such as 'my skills are out of date', 'there are no jobs out there in a recession', 'the children need me at home', 'the house will be a mess if I go out to work', when really what is holding them back is a lack of confidence.

Parenthood has an amazing ability to zap confidence from a woman. Bringing up children should be a time when we have lots to be proud of. Just surviving through a whole day with two small children without any major mishaps occurring to me always felt like a big achievement. Yet the world at large doesn't seem to value the role. We quickly feel out of touch with the workplace and start to believe that we can't do the things which only a few months previously seemed no problem. While for many women it can be a positive, conscious decision to stay at home with children for several years, for others it can become easier and easier to put off going back to work because of a fear of what has quickly become 'the unknown'.

> I had a balance of both positive and negative reaction from people when they were aware that I was not in paid work. It was far easier to pick up and run with the negative, as the role of 'lone parent' still seems to carry a 'stigma', whereby an individual's personal circumstance is not always considered or perhaps assumptions are made. This can compound any feelings of anxiety or 'shame' associated with not being financially independent or an employed member of the community.
>
> Anna

> It's been horrible not working, a real struggle. The whole money thing has been really difficult. It's totally sapped my self-esteem and confidence.
>
> Deborah

One approach to looking at improving confidence is firstly to find ways of improving our positive thinking and secondly to work on reducing our negative thinking. We will look at each in turn.

Improving positive thinking - try some of the following activities:

Roles in life

It is so easy when asked 'what do you do?' at a party or other event to say 'oh, I'm just a mum'. Jot down some of the roles that you carry out on a day to day basis in your life as a parent, such as: partner, mother, teacher, counsellor, gardener, taxi driver, party planner, morality trainer, nutritionist or cook; you will be able to add many more to this. Now have a think about the skills involved in carrying out each of those roles: caring, explaining, communicating, listening, driving, organising etc. You may be surprised at the number of things you are responsible for and the many skills involved in carrying out these everyday tasks. We'll come back to this in the next chapter.

Have a think about some of the following questions:
- What adjectives would friends use to describe you?
- Have you taken responsibility for something or organised an event that went really well?
- What difficulties in your life (illness, bereavement, separation) have you come through? What have you learnt from this experience?
- Describe something you have made or designed that you are proud of.
- Think about an achievement that you are proud of. Try to remember how that felt.

Look after yourself

As a parent, the children's needs often tend to come first and our own needs can easily get forgotten. Looking after ourselves is an essential part of being a good parent. We need to show our children that we matter and have needs and are not just there to be a slave to them, however much it may feel like that. Caring for our own physical and mental health will enable us to have the energy and resources to be good a parent, as well as being good role models for our children's health. Try to take on board some of the following tips:
- Eat healthily.
- Get a good night's sleep if you can (or at least make sure your partner or a friend look after the children so that you can sleep).
- Get regular exercise, even if the only way you can do that is to go for long walks with the pushchair or doing an exercise video when the children are in bed.

- Find time for yourself once a week, could your partner or a friend look after the children one evening a week, so that you can go to an evening class, go out for a drink with friends or go to the cinema? If not, go to bed early with a good book or have a long bath with candles or a glass of wine.
- Take care of your appearance. Looks aren't everything, but it's amazing what a confidence boost it is when you make an effort and someone compliments you. If you can afford to, get your hair cut or buy a new outfit occasionally. Maybe just once a week, make an effort to wear something that you know you look good in, even if it is just to take the children to school, followed by a trip round the supermarket.

Self-affirmation

Self-affirmations are statements we make about ourselves, to ourselves on a regular basis, in the belief that if we say it enough it will come true. It can help to balance out negative thoughts that we get from ourselves and from others. It can help us to aim towards a goal of something we want to be or become.

They could include some of the following:
- I am confident
- I am talented
- I am a good parent
- I can lose weight
- I can work and manage at home
- I will praise my children today
- I will control my temper today

Or whatever it is you want to work on and to believe.

You could write one or two statements on a post-it note and stick it on your mirror, on the fridge, or on the steering wheel in the car. Repeat these statements to yourself whenever you see them - saying it in front of the mirror can help. The more you say it, the more you will start to believe it.

Dealing with negative thinking

What is negative thinking?

So hopefully if you have worked through some of the above activities you will be full of positive thoughts and maybe starting to feel better about yourself. Now you need to deal with some of the negative thoughts which are working to cancel them out. Negative thinking can come from so many places, often stemming from childhood. They can be as a result of criticism, bullying or discrimination. They may come from past failure or from society or the media telling us we should look a certain way, or that we shouldn't boast about ourselves. Examples of negative thinking might include:

- If only I had …. then I would be OK
- I'm useless at ….
- I can't …..
- I couldn't do …. because ….
- I'm a failure, there's no point trying
- People like me can't do things like that
- I never …… I always ….

We may have learnt negative thoughts from others:

- You couldn't do that
- You're bound to fail at that, why try?
- You're useless

Negative thoughts can go on in our heads all the time, often subconsciously. Maybe you make negative comments to yourself such as: 'I am clumsy' or 'I am disorganised'. Maybe you respond negatively to compliments about your appearance: 'oh it's just something old I threw on in a hurry'. Or maybe you constantly compare yourself to others, or make negative comments about things or people. Recognising these negative thoughts and trying to stop them, can have a huge effect on our confidence.

Try spending a day consciously thinking about all the negative things that you say, or that go unspoken in your head. Try writing these down, you might be surprised by what you see. Could you think of some positive thoughts or comments to replace the negative ones? Spend a week trying to replace your negative thoughts and comments with positive ones. It will make a huge difference to how you feel about yourself but will also change how people respond to you.

Negative beliefs

Negative thinking can be in the form of negative beliefs. When you start to analyse these beliefs you realise that they are probably untrue. Beware of any statement that starts 'always' or 'never', such as 'I always fail at job interviews', or 'I never get quiz questions right'. These beliefs, once identified, will generally turn out not to be true in all cases.

I have a tendency to believe that everyone with a trolley in a supermarket is out to get me and therefore deliberately obstructs my route at every possibility. Not surprisingly, this can make me get quite angry and frustrated in the supermarket. Once I had identified this negative belief, I realised that it is not true, but that people are generally in a world of their own, and occasionally perhaps a little thoughtless, it's not personal. With this newly formed belief, I can handle the supermarket in a more positive and accepting frame of mind.

Try to identify some of your negative beliefs. Can you replace them with something more realistic and positive?

Dealing with anger and resentment
We've all been hurt by other people at some point in our lives. Whether it is criticism, being let down by a friend, gossip in the playground, not getting the invitation you were hoping for, or much worse, it can lead to anger and resentment. Holding on to this anger and resentment will harm ourselves far more than the person we are holding it against. It may not be easy, but try to let go of past hurts and move on, for your own sake. Learn to manage your anger and to give and receive criticism in a constructive and assertive way. See Chapter Thirteen for more on this.

Dealing with our fears
Often what holds us back is a fear of failure. Susan Jeffrey's book: 'Feel The Fear and Do It Anyway' is a fascinating look at fear and how it debilitates us[22]. Her belief is that our fears will only go away when we attempt the thing that we have the most fear of and that pushing through the fear and attempting the thing we are most scared of is less frightening than living with the helplessness we would otherwise have. She challenges us to question how likely our fears are to come true; in reality most of them probably won't! If they do come true, she shows that the chances are we will have the resilience to come through them and to learn from them:

> `All you have to do to diminish your fear is to develop more trust in your ability to handle whatever comes your way.'
>
> Susan Jeffers – Feel the Fear and Do It Anyway [2]

A challenging book which is well worth a read.

As you start to feel more confident on the inside, you will start to exude confidence on the outside. People will notice this and respond to you in a more positive way and have confidence in you. In turn this will increase your confidence in yourself, leading to a virtuous circle of confidence improvement. This is known as the 'Cycle of Confidence':

The Cycle of Confidence

Your
Confidence
Is Increased

You are
Confident

People Have
Confidence
In You

A few more confidence boosters:

- Like and accept yourself - others do, why can't you too?
- Spend time with friends and people who make you feel positive about yourself.
- Be nice to people; smile or say hello to strangers or a lonely person at the bus stop, pay compliments to people or help someone out when they are in need. It will make them feel better, but it will make you feel great too.
- Change something, try to make the world a better place, write to your M.P. about something that matters to you or support a charity you believe in.
- Imagine succeeding with your goals, how would this feel?
- Complete things you've been meaning to get on with for months.
- Start a conversation with someone you wouldn't normally talk to.
- Respect yourself – stand up for your opinions and beliefs and so 'no' every now and then. (See Chapter Thirteen

for more on assertiveness).

- Set yourself goals and reward yourself when you achieve them.
- Try something new - start a new activity or evening class
- Pamper yourself because 'you are worth it'!

'I can't believe that there are any heights that can't be scaled by a man [sic] who knows the secrets of making dreams come true. This special secret, it seems to me, can be summarized in four C s. They are curiosity, confidence, courage, and constancy, and the greatest of all is confidence.'

Walt Disney

Points to ponder

- It is unusual to find a mum who doesn't lack self-confidence after a period of time at home with children.
- Don't let your lack of confidence stop you doing what you want to do with your life.
- Be proud of what you have achieved and learnt in spending time with your children.
- Look after yourself.
- Try some positive affirmations.
- Challenge yourself to try something new even if it scares you.
- Be aware of negative thoughts holding you back. Recognise them and change them.

Reading

Gael Lindenfield, *Super Confidence,* Element, 2000

Gael Lindenfield, *Managing Anger,* Element, 2000

Susan Jeffers, *Feel the Fear and Do It Anyway,* Vermillion, 2007

Chapter Four

What can I do?
Finding a career that's right for you

If you are qualified and experienced in a particular career area and have enjoyed that line of work, the chances are that you will want to return to this field. If so, you might like to skip to the next chapter. For some women however, it may not be feasible to return to a previous line of work. Perhaps the demands of commuting or travelling abroad will no longer fit in with family life. Maybe you were dissatisfied with your work before having children, or maybe becoming a parent has inspired you to think about a change of direction. This could be a good time reconsider what you want to be doing, even if the conclusion is that you were in the right line of work to start with!

'Change is scary because the brain naturally finds it easier to repeat the same patterns and habits and it takes more effort to create new neural pathways. Work is such a huge part of people's lives. It affects their identities, financial situation and future prospects, confidence, perceived status and emotional and financial security.'

www.liberateyourtalent.com [1]

So how do you decide what career would be right for you? This will be one of the biggest challenges you face in your return to work and is not an easy process; but get it right and you will be glad you put the effort in. If you are going on a journey, a map will be useless to you unless you know where you are starting from, where you are trying to get to and how you are going to get there. Career planning is a little like a journey, you need to start by knowing yourself, what kind of person you are and what your skills, interests and values are. This is your starting to point to begin exploring the options available to you and narrowing that down to a clear idea of where you want to be career-wise. Only then can you think about how to get there; this will involve finding out what training you need to do and what skills you need to develop, as well as starting to look at the job hunting skills which we will address in the next few chapters.

Too often I see clients who come in wanting help with their CV, when they are not really sure what they want to do. I gently encourage them to take a step back and think about where they are now and where they are trying to get to, before starting on the journey of trying to get there.

So the process really involves doing a life and work audit; evaluating yourself and the world-of-work and putting the results together to find the perfect match. So to start off there are a number of questions you need to ask yourself which I will go through one by one. I suggest you take some time over this process, talking about it to people who know you well and jotting down thoughts and ideas as they come to you.

1.   What can I offer?

This is really about looking at your skills, experience and knowledge and thinking about what you have to offer an employer.

A skill is basically something which you can do well, and in this context we are mainly talking about skills that you enjoy using. We all have a wide range of skills, but often aren't aware of many of them, or lack confidence in the skills we have, perhaps because we haven't used them for some time.

Try making a list of skills that you have and add to it every time you think of something new. To demonstrate to an employer that you have a skill you will need to evidence it with a qualification or an example of something you have done that demonstrates that skill in action. As mentioned in the previous chapter, examples can be taken from work, home, voluntary work or studying. For example organising a school fair might demonstrate skills in organisation, management, delegation, marketing, negotiation, budgeting, time management, to name a few. Ask friends and family members what they think you are good at, as they may recognise things which you are not aware of.

Think about skills you have used and developed as a parent. In an average day looking after children, we might be involved in a whole range of activities all of which involve using different skills:

Activity	Skill used
Helping with homework	Teaching, explaining
Going to the supermarket	Budgeting, planning
Dealing with a toddler tantrum	Negotiation, assertiveness, communication
Asking a child to tidy their bedroom	Delegation, assertiveness, persuading
Supporting a child through bullying	Listening, counselling, problem solving, negotiation with teachers
Planning a holiday	Researching, record keeping, planning, budgeting, consultation, decision making

Some of these skills may not seem relevant, but skills learnt in one context, perhaps in the home, may be useful in another context, such as the workplace. These are transferable skills; more on this later. Have a look back at the section on 'roles in life' in the previous chapter to prompt you further.

Look at your experience as well. Make a list of projects you have been involved with at work and at home, voluntary activities you have helped with, groups that you are part of and hobbies that you take part in.

What specialist knowledge do you have, which perhaps the average person doesn't have? You may have a particular understanding of certain issues from your previous work or studying, or maybe you've developed an awareness of child development from being a parent or a specialised knowledge of your local area.

If at this stage you are struggling to find things to write down, this could be due to a lack of confidence. Talk to friends, who might be quick to point out skills you didn't realise you had or have another look at Chapter Three on Confidence Building. Or perhaps you need to go back to Chapter Two and think about things you could be doing now to build up the skills, experience and knowledge you may need to find a job.

What is your USP (Unique Selling Point)? What are your strengths that make you different from others? What makes you stand out from the crowd?

2.   What do I want from work?

The things we hope to gain from working may include: job satisfaction, financial rewards and other benefits, status, sense of identity and self-esteem, the right kind of employer, something that fits in with the family.

Ask yourself what you like doing in terms of work activities and what gives you job satisfaction? Your answers might include:
- Being an expert in your area of knowledge.
- Sharing information with people or teaching someone a new skill.
- Being creative and making or designing new things or maybe solving technical problems.
- Supporting someone who is struggling and helping them to move forward in their life.
- Selling things, being goal-oriented and meeting targets.

Have a think about jobs, projects or activities you have been involved with in the past (either at work or home). Which things have you enjoyed the most? What things have you looked forward to doing and which activities have you dreaded or made you clock-watch with boredom? Have you ever got to the end of the day and felt really pleased with yourself, that you've done a good day's work? If so, why was that, what were you doing?

These answers relate to your answers to question 1, the things you are good at (your skills) will often (but not always) be the things that give you the most satisfaction.

What kind of environment do you like to work in?
- Do you like being outdoors and active or on a computer in an office?
- Do you like working on your own or in a team environment?
- Do you want to be working with members of the public and customers or primarily with colleagues from your own organisation?

What kind of organisation do you want to work for?
- A big one with opportunities for promotion and training or a small one where you can be a big fish in a small pond?
- Do you want to work in the public, private or voluntary sector with the different values and benefits which go with them?

What kind of salary and benefits package are you after? Think carefully about the difference between what you need and what you may want.

3.   What are my values?

What matters to you in life? Do you live to work or work to live? Are you purely after financial reward to fund a life of luxury or do you work simply for the satisfaction that work gives you, with no regard for financial gain? Two extremes, I know, but most of us will fall somewhere in between. Where do you fit on the continuum?

Where does work fit into your life? This is something that changes over time and may well be different for you now that you have a family. You may want time and energy to spend with your children at the end of a day's work, or you may want to ensure financial security for your children's future and the choices which that brings.

What do you want to achieve in life? Look at your life backwards. When you are 70 or 80, what would you like to be able to look back on and be proud of?

> A colleague of mine is proud of her great great grandmother, who alongside bringing up nine children, set up committees to tackle child poverty in Glasgow in the 1920s and was involved in setting up the first health visiting programmes in the country. A friend of mine is proud of her Mum because she was always there for her when she got home from school and sacrificed a lot to take her to several swimming training sessions a week.

What would you like your children to be proud of you for? How are you going to achieve that?

We are all different and have different values, none of them right or wrong, just different. What really matters to you?

I realise that at this stage I am asking more questions than I am answering. This section is about YOU and you will need to work hard to build up a picture of yourself, what you have to offer and what you want from life. It will take time and is an ongoing process which you can add to. You will find a number of resources online to help you to identify your skills and interests. You might like to start by looking at the government website nextstep.direct.gov.uk and having a go at the 'Skills Health Check'. This includes a section on 'What's Important to You'.

So far you've started to look at you, now you need to go and look at the world of work and find out what is out there. Start looking at employment opportunities in relation to what you have learnt about yourself.

4.   What does work offer?

In question 2, you thought about what you wanted from work; now start to look at jobs and careers in terms of what they offer. If you want a job that involves caring for people, think about the kinds of jobs which involve this. If you want to work for a company that looks after its staff, offers plenty of perks and gives opportunities for promotion and training - which employers are likely to offer this? Have a look at 'The Times Online 100 Best Companies to Work For'[2] for some ideas. Find out more about job families and particular jobs that might interest you. Have a look at the 'Job Profiles' section of nextstep.direct.gov.uk for information on what activities might be involved in different jobs, the skills and interests required and the type of training needed.

5.   What does work demand?

In question 1, you thought about what you had to offer employers in terms of your skills, experience and knowledge. Which employers and career areas might want what you have to offer?

Look in the local or national papers and vacancy websites to see what kind of jobs are around. What are employers asking for? Identify jobs which may use your skills. You could look at person specifications for different jobs online to find out what employers are looking for. Have a brainstorm of jobs that might require someone with your profile. Find out as much as you can about jobs you think of and talk to friends or contacts who do those jobs to find out more. Does the job offer what you want and ask for what you have to offer?

Brainstorm different career ideas, write lots of ideas down on a piece of paper and don't worry for now how ridiculous they may seem. Write down some pros and cons for each job and start to prioritise them. Do more research into these jobs, always bearing in mind the previous questions, 'what do I want from work?' and 'what so I have to offer to employers?'

If you come up with jobs that are asking for more than you have to offer, could you do further training or get some more experience by doing voluntary work?

6. Am I being realistic?

So your research has inspired you to consider being a marine biologist, but you live in Birmingham 100 miles from the sea. Is this realistic? Maybe not, unless you and your family are prepared to move, which may not be an option for you right now.

Or perhaps you've decided that you want to train to be a counsellor. Is there a demand for counsellors in your area or is the community you live in swamped with them? Even if your area is swamped with them, it doesn't mean that you shouldn't aim to be a counsellor, but go into it with your eyes open and know that competition for jobs may be hard.

Finding up-to-date labour market information will be vital to help you know whether there is a demand or an oversupply of skilled staff in the area you are interested in. The following websites may be useful to look at:
- www.nomisweb.co.uk
- www.careersbox.co.uk has videos of employees and employers talking about their work.
- www.skillclear.co.uk gives an up-to-date list of government approved jobs with a skills shortage, which is used for immigration purposes. You may not be an immigrant, but it gives a useful guide as to which areas might be worth training in.
- www.monster.co.uk has an interesting 'occupational trends' section, including a monthly 'UK Employment Index' showing job availability in different sectors by region.

Remember to talk to people who work in the field you are interested in to get a fuller picture. Statistics can be quite dry and don't always tell the whole story.

How realistic you want to be will be related to how much of a risk-taker you are. If you like taking risks, the chances are that you will be more prepared to go for something that doesn't appear on the surface to be hugely realistic, but are prepared to take a chance. Always make sure you've got a good back up plan though.

Putting it all together

I hope that having worked through these questions you will be starting to get an idea of the type of job you might like to do. It's hard to answer each of the questions in isolation and you will need to go backwards and forwards between them as they are all interrelated. It's rather like doing a jigsaw, first you need to know what shape the piece is, that's you. Next you need to find the right shaped space to fit it, that's your perfect job.

Talk your ideas through with friends and family, particularly people you know will be honest with you. It can be hard to narrow your ideas down to just one job, and it may not be sensible to either. You may want to start by applying for a range of jobs. You will soon get a feel for the ones which are most realistic for you.

Other thoughts to help you on your way

Be creative in your search and think about your transferable skills. A transferable skill is one which you have learnt and used in one setting, but could use in an entirely different context.

Michelle was a secondary school teacher who loved the classroom but felt that the marking and preparation workload put too much strain on family life. She identified clear communication as the main skill that she used in teaching, as she enjoyed finding simple and appropriate ways to make an idea understandable to her teenage audience. She realised that this was a skill she could use in marketing and public relations. After working for a public relations company for a while, she then set up her own agency which specialises in community-related communications.

Could you move sideways in your current or previous career? If you teach young children, could you move into teaching adults with basic literacy needs or English to speakers of other languages? If you are an engineer who has moved into a sales and marketing role in the company, could you do sales and marketing in another sector? Or perhaps you could stay in the same career but work in a different context? If you are a qualified accountant with experience in the private sector, could you work as an accountant in the public or voluntary sectors?

Does your work lend itself to working on a freelance or consultancy basis? Or perhaps you could consider setting up your own business. More on this in the next chapter!

There is lots of support and advice available for anyone who wants help in identifying a career route. Contact your local branch of the Next Step adult careers service for an appointment with a Careers Adviser or ring the national Careers Advice Service helpline for similar support over the phone. You will find other careers guidance practitioners in the Yellow Pages.

Dream dreams

Despite what I said earlier about adding a healthy dose of realism to your ideas, I like to encourage people to dream dreams and think big. What is your vision of the future? Only you can make it happen……..

Find a quiet place to sit, shut your eyes and spend a few minutes letting your imagination run free. Try to imagine how you would like a day in your life to be in ten years time. Who would you be with? Where would you be? What would you be doing? Forget all the barriers of everyday life that limit your imagination and be positive and optimistic. Then, draw a picture of yourself, or jot down words or phrases that describe your new life. Make it as detailed as possible. What's good about the life you have imagined and why? How do you feel about your life?

OK, now come back down to earth. So travelling around the world for a year might not be realistic when you still have children at home. Perhaps you don't have the million pounds you need to buy that organic hill farm in Wales, where you can live self sufficiently, running a little tea shop from the front room of your thatched farm house. But are there small parts of your dream that could become a reality? Could you save up enough money or sell something to go on a really interesting holiday with the children? Or could you get an allotment near to home and start growing your own vegetables? Could your ideas inspire a completely new career you hadn't thought of before?

> 'Risk is the tariff for leaving the land of predictable misery'
>
> Howard Figler

Changes in the world of work

The world of work is changing at a fast pace. It may have been a number of years since you were last in paid work and you may be concerned that your skills are out of date and you will feel out of your depth. You need to know about these changes so that you are prepared for them. Think about going on a training course (particularly in IT) or doing some work experience to build your confidence. Some facts for you:

- Between 1971 and 2008, women's employment levels increased from 56% to 70%, while men's employment fell from 92% to 78%.[3]
- The economic downturn of 2008 impacted less on women's employment than on men's.[4]
- One fifth of women in employment do administrative or secretarial work, compared to 4% of men.[5]
- 42% of working women work part-time compared to 12% of men.[6]

- Women who work part-time earn 41% less per hour than men who work full time.[7]
- Email and the internet are commonplace in work places.
- A 'job for life' is now a rarity, we can expect to have several careers and many different jobs throughout our lifetime.
- Organisations are now more likely to take on part-time workers and contract out work to freelancers
- Flexible working patterns such as job-sharing, term-time only working, flexitime and other family-friendly policies are on the increase.
- Employees need to adopt a 'life-long learning' approach to keeping skills updated throughout their working life.
- 'Women are crowded into a narrow range of lower-paying occupations, mainly those available part-time, that do not make the best use of their skills.'[7]
- 'The top five 'recession proof' jobs are thought to be: plumbing, IT, midwifery (or indeed any nursing or health care job), teaching and public relations'.[8]

> 'I created what I call 'a portfolio life', setting aside 100 days a year for making money, 100 days for writing, 50 days for what I consider good works, and 100 days for spending time with my wife'
>
> Charles Handy

Points to ponder

- Don't be scared to reinvent yourself, now could be a good time to re-evaluate and change your career.
- Get a friend to help you write a list of your skills, you probably have more than you realise.
- Don't forget about transferable skills.
- Ask for help in working out what to do – make an appointment with a careers adviser.
- Find out as much as you can about careers you are considering.
- The workplace may have changed since you last worked. Make sure you keep up to date.
- Don't be scared to have big dreams, but make sure they are tempered with a pinch of reality.

Information

Labour market information	www.nomisweb.co.uk
Videos of employees and employers talking about their work.	www.careersbox.co.uk
Up-to-date list of government approved jobs with a skills shortage, which is used for immigration purposes.	www.skillclear.co.uk
Occupational trends	www.monster.co.uk
Next Step adult careers service	nextstep.direct.gov.uk government funded careers information, advice and guidance
Next Step freephone careers advice service	www.careersadvice.direct.gov.uk/ or call 0800 100 900
Various tools including 'Skills and Interests Assessment', 'Career Values', 'CV builder', 'Job Profiles' and 'Funding Directory'.	nextstep.direct.gov.uk

Reading

Barry Hopson and Mike Scally, *Build Your Own Rainbow: A Workbook For Career and Life Management,* Management Books 2000 Ltd, 2009.

Richard Nelson Bolles, *What Color is Your Parachute? 2010: A Practical Manual for Job-Hunters and Career-Changers,* Ten Speed Press, 2010.

John Lees, *How to Get a Job You'll Love, 2009/10 Edition: A Practical Guide to Unlocking Your Talents and Finding Your Ideal Career,* McGraw-Hill Professional, 2008.

Chapter Five

Working for yourself –
Be your own boss

For many women, trying to find work that fits in with family life can seem all but impossible (although read Chapter Ten on flexible working). One solution to this is to be your own boss. Maybe you could do some freelance work, or consultancy. Perhaps you have a fantastic idea to set up a business or social enterprise. Or maybe you could be employed by someone else to work hours to suit you, from your own home. In this chapter we will consider the different options, look at the pros and cons of each one and look at pointers for further information.

Freelance work and other working from home jobs

Start with what you can do already. Does your previous career lend itself to freelance work? How about contacting your former employer and asking if they have any pieces of work you could do from home, perhaps working on a research project or writing a funding bid. Or could you seek out other clients you could work for? A number of careers lend themselves to freelance work such as editing, writing, graphic design, website design, marketing, administrative work, one-to-one teaching or tutoring. Or you might want to try something new such as proofreading or bookkeeping. There are many courses available to prepare you for these kinds of roles.

Start a business

Perhaps you have a fantastic idea to start a business. Make sure you have a really good product or service to offer. Do some market research, and find out if there is a demand for your product at the price you want to charge. Will you need premises, staff or other services? Will you need to get a loan or some investment to get started?

The subject of starting a business warrants a whole book on its own (and there are plenty out there), but there is lots of support available to anyone who may want to start up a business.

Business Link operates across the country and provides free information, advice and support on setting up a business. They run courses, workshops and networking events and can help with writing a business plan, sourcing funding and how to market your business. There may be a local business network or sometimes a business women's network you could join for networking and support.

Sally Wilkins – Designer of the 'Wilkinet Baby Carrier'
It was out of Sally's frustration with commercially available baby carriers that she designed the well know 'Wilkinet' baby carrier after her fourth child was born. Initially something she produced for her own family and then friends, it soon became a small business based around the kitchen table of her small cottage. In time, the Wilkinet grew to become one of the UK's best selling baby carriers.

Don't underestimate the time, energy and funding required in starting a business. Although you may choose this option so that you can work hours to suit you and spend time with your children, it can be all consuming and may take up every waking hour, at least to start with. It may also be a year or more before you can take any money out of the business and it is a sad fact that over 50% of small businesses fail in the first year.

Although working long hours at times, running my own company gives me a greater degree of flexibility to fit with family commitments and a very high level of job satisfaction.

Michelle

Social Enterprise

Another option which is becoming increasingly popular among people interested in business who also want to make a difference in the world, is to set up or participate in a social enterprise. Many mums have started social or community projects before going back to work, often motivated by the needs they have identified while pregnant or with young children. One example is a business promoting recyclable nappies. Social enterprises are a cross between charities and businesses, and they can be exciting as well as sympathetic and flexible places to work. They can also be collaborative projects where a group of people decide to address a particular need together. If you don't feel you can set up your own, maybe look for a job with an existing one in your area; they often spin off new business ideas, and perhaps that will be your chance. Check out www.socialenterprise.org.uk for more information and inspiration.

Franchises

Franchising can be a great way to start a business without having to come up with a completely original idea and with possibly less risk. A franchise is basically a tried and tested business model and name that you buy from a parent company. You have a licence to operate the franchise within a particular area and to use the company name and branding. Usually a franchise comes with support and training, depending on the package. Well known franchise brands include Clark's Shoes and Domino's Pizzas, but could also be much smaller concerns such as a small local magazine, pre-school music class or maths tuition programme.

To set up a franchise you would need to pay an initial fee to the franchisor and then an ongoing management fee, often a percentage of your turnover. In return you get training, product development, support, advice and possibly national advertising. The British Franchise Association provides lots of information and advice about setting up a franchise, as well as a list of accredited members.

Direct selling (network marketing or multi-level marketing)

Direct selling involves using your networks to sell a product in return for a commission. This idea has been around for years in the form of Avon (ladies) and Tupperware parties. These days there are hundreds of products you can sell including children's books, greetings cards, kitchen products, clothes, toiletries or jewellery. The usual model is that you buy a set of products from the company, which you then demonstrate to a group of people, often in their own home in a 'party' setting. You take orders and receive commission on the sales made. Ideally one of your clients will then host a party themselves with their own set of friends, thus increasing your network.

Direct selling becomes multi-level marketing when you support someone else to set up a direct selling network themselves. You then receive a commission on their sales as well as your own, in return for providing them with support.

It is basically a sales job. To succeed, you need to believe in the product you are selling and be able to convince others in the product too. It is a flexible option, enabling you to take on as little or as much as you want, depending on your circumstances. Bear in mind that work may well be predominantly (although not exclusively) in the evenings, which may or may not suit you.

Network marketing has had some bad press and some companies have been known to give exaggerated claims as to how much could be earned. Make sure you do some research, use a reputable, well-known company and talk to others who have done it, before jumping in. The Direct Selling Association provides lots of useful advice and information, as well as a list of members who sign up to their code of practice.

Other types of homeworking

There are plenty of opportunities to be employed by someone else to work from home. This could include delivering catalogues or phone books, or doing some kind of practical work at home such as sewing or making up envelopes. Many of these opportunities are genuine, but there are many scams around where you have to send off money for a starter pack and get nothing in return. www.homeworkinguk.com offers advice on how to avoid scams as well as some suggestions of reputable companies to try.

Childminding

One option which many women consider is to become a childminder. There are now 67,000 registered childminders in the UK. Childminding enables you to work for yourself, from home, potentially looking after your own children at the same time as being paid to look after others'. You can find out more from the National Childminding Association or arrange to go on a pre-registration session provided by your local authority – contact your

Families Information Service for more details. If you enjoy looking after children, then this could be a good option for you.

Other ideas might include:

- Buying and selling products through online auction shops.
- Training as a counsellor or life coach and working from home.
- Making craft products to sell online.
- Cleaning, ironing, gardening or dog walking for other people.
- Setting up a bed and breakfast in your home.

Advantages of working for yourself:

- You get to choose the hours you work.
- You make your own decisions and don't have to answer to a senior manager.
- You get the satisfaction of having achieved something.
- You may (or may not) earn more than working for someone else.
- You can say 'no' to work you don't want to do.

Disadvantages of working for yourself:

- You may have to work many more hours than you would like, particularly at the beginning.
- Your income could be unpredictable (or even non-existent).
- You will need to keep accurate records of income and expenses for tax purposes.
- You don't get sick pay, holiday pay or maternity leave.
- If you are working on your own, you may get lonely and miss the company of colleagues.
- If you are working at home, you may get distracted by callers or piles of housework that you know need doing.

Points to ponder

- Self-employment may be the route to following your dream and give you the flexibility you need.
- Running a business can take up huge amounts of time.
- A franchise may offer you the support you need to make your business work.
- Beware of homeworking scams and 'get rich quick' promises.

- Let your home insurer know that you are working from home and contact the Inland Revenue for advice about income tax.
- Get as much help as you can – go on a business start-up course and speak to Business Link for advice.

Information

Freelancer's Network	www.freelancers.net
Business Link	www.businesslink.gov.uk
Business networks	www.business-network.co.uk
Women in Business	www.wibn.co.uk
The Social Enterprise Coalition	www.socialenterprise.org.uk
The Franchise Association	www.thebfa.org
The Direct Selling Association	www.dsa.org.uk
Information on homeworking	www.homeworking.co.uk or www.homeworkinguk.com
Families Information Service	www.familyinformationservices.org.uk
National Childminding Association	www.ncma.org.uk
The Inland Revenue	www.hmrc.gov.uk

Reading

Judy Heminsley, *Work from Home: How to Make Money Working at Home - and Get the Most Out of Life,* How to Books Ltd, 2009

Antonia Chitty and Roni Jay, *Family Friendly Working: Inspiring Ideas for Making Money When You Have Kids,* White Ladder, 2008

Sara Williams, *The 'Financial Times' Guide to Business Start Up 2010,* Financial Times / Prentice Hall, 2009

Martin Clark, *The Social Entrepreneur Revolution,* Marshall Cavendish, 2009

Chapter Six

Where to find a job

So you've thought about your skills and interests and hopefully by now you have an idea of the type of job you would like to look for. Now, how are you going to find that job? You need to adopt a range of strategies to identify suitable jobs to apply for. It is generally estimated that only 30% of jobs that are filled are ever advertised in newspapers, journals or the internet. The remaining 70%, commonly known as 'hidden jobs' will be filled by people who make a direct, speculative approach to employers, filled internally, by head-hunting, or by people whose previous application for a job has been kept on file. You need to ensure that your job search covers both advertised and hidden jobs. Do this by making speculative approaches to employers, using employment agencies and by networking.

Here are a few ideas to help with your search:

Newspapers: your local paper is a good place to start looking for jobs, or to just give you an idea of the types of jobs around. It can be incredibly expensive, especially for small employers, to advertise in a local paper, so don't assume that all jobs available will be advertised here. National papers may also be a good place to look. Many papers will advertise sector specific jobs on different days.

Employment Agencies: these deal with a wide range of vacancies, both temporary and permanent. It may well be worth registering with several agencies to increase your chances. Remember that you are not the client, but the employer is; the agency's job is finding employees for its clients and not primarily to support you in finding work. That's not to say that they won't be helpful, as many agencies will be very supportive and offer invaluable advice, but don't be too surprised if they turn you away because you don't suit the profile of staff they are looking for, or because your childcare needs constrain your options. www.agencycentral.co.uk enables you to search for local employment agencies offering work in different sectors. It also shows whether agencies offer part-time or job share positions.

Slivers of Time: this is a recent public sector approach to finding temporary work for job seekers, working quite differently from the average employment agency. 'Work seekers' run an online diary of availability, while employers search for workers by skill and availability, ranked by reliability and hourly rate. As with other employment agencies, ad-hoc temporary work may not suit you if need to make child care arrangements at short notice for pre-school children. However, if your children are school age and you can find work to fit, this could be an excellent introduction back into the world of work. www.sliversoftime.com

Professional and trade journals relevant to your career area will be available in your local library or vacancies may be available online.

Business directories: Your local Directory of Commerce and Industry should be available from your local library or online from your local Chamber of Commerce website. This is an excellent source of information on local companies to assist you with a speculative search for jobs. Visit www.britishchambers.org.uk to search for your local chamber and online directory of commerce and industry.

Internet: In recent years the internet has been a rapidly expanding resource for job hunting. I don't think this is the place to review the many different sites, but just putting 'job search' into a search engine will bring up the most popular ones. You will also find many local and sector specific websites to use as well. Many of these sites also give you the opportunity to upload your CV, so that you have the chance to come up on employers' searches.

Put your CV online: Lots of jobsearch websites allow you to upload your CV allowing employers and recruiters to search for candidates using certain keywords. Make sure your CV uses keywords appropriate to your field, so that your CV pops up high up on a search.

Employers: if you know of particular employers you would like to work for, look at their website regularly for vacancies. In some cases, it may be worth going into the organisation and asking about vacancies or looking at their vacancy notice boards. This is particularly the case in the retail sector. In the case of some larger employers you may be able to register for regular email notifications of vacancies.

Previous employers: if you had a good experience with any of your previous employers, consider contacting them about any opportunities they may have. They will know you well and hopefully know that you can do the job. You would have the advantage of going back into a familiar environment.

Networking: make use of any contacts you have. Make it known that you are looking for work. Mention it in passing to parents you meet in the playground or someone you meet at a party. Talk to friends and ask them to let you know if anything comes up in the organisation they work for, or ask for an introduction to their boss. Make it a habit to ask people about their job and how they got into it. Find out about networking meetings you could join - it could be a local business network, or a network of people who work in a particular sector or for different organisations in your locality. Many network groups will send out regular emails or newsletters, often with vacancy details.

Voluntary work: as mentioned in the previous chapter, this can be an excellent way of developing your skills and building your confidence whilst giving you something else to put on your CV. In some cases it can lead into paid employment in that organisation. Being a volunteer may also make you eligible to apply for any internally advertised vacancies. Contact your local Volunteer Service to find out about opportunities or use www.do-it.org.uk

Jobcentre Plus: whether you are in receipt of benefits or not, anyone can go into their Jobcentre to look at the vacancy notice boards. However, you may find it easier to look at their website: jobseekers.direct.gov.uk

How to decide which jobs to apply for

Make sure you are selective in the jobs you apply for and do a few good quality applications, rather than lots of poor ones. You may only find one job every week or so to apply for, which may be manageable. If, however, you are finding lots of jobs to apply for, be selective. Consider the following:
- Will this job suit me, will I find it interesting, will I enjoy it and will it challenge me?
- Will it fit in with my personal circumstances; are they likely to offer me the flexible working options I need?
- Does it pay the kind of salary I want/expect/need?
- Look at the person specification; do I have the skills and experience they are looking for?
- Start off by being choosy and aim high; you can always lower your sights if you are unsuccessful.

- Maybe you will have a better chance of going for something at a lower level, build some confidence, prove yourself and hope for promotion.
- Don't be put off if you don't have all the 'essential' criteria if you feel you make up for it elsewhere. Maybe no one will meet all the criteria and the employer will have to compromise:

Research shows that women don't tend to apply for jobs because they don't feel they fit all the criteria exactly, whereas men are more likely to adopt the opposite attitude[1]. So, if you've got one of the requirements mentioned, it's worth a try. Have a go anyway and you may surprise yourself by getting the job and then finding that you are good at it!

It may seem obvious, but do keep records of jobs you apply for. It's worth keeping the original advert (and a note of where you saw it), the job description and person specification as well as a copy of the application you sent off, whether CV or application form. It could be helpful to make a chart to show what stage you have got to with each job. You may want to follow up applications with a phone call or email if you haven't heard anything a couple of weeks after the closing date. Keeping your application will make it so much easier if you get invited for interview, as you know what the employer has in front of them. Also, while each application or CV needs to be tailored to the individual job you are applying for, looking back at previous applications will be a useful reminder of projects you have worked on or good phrases you have used.

Keeping a file of your applications and a table like the one shown on the next page may help you to keep your applications organised.

Points to ponder

- Don't underestimate the power of networking and using contacts.
- Have a go at those jobs that seem out of your range, you may just be lucky!
- Be prepared to take what you can, that first step on the ladder could act as your launch pad.
- Be organised in your approach to job hunting, keep records of everything you do.

Job Title	Employer contact details	Where & when vacancy seen	Date application returned	Copy taken	Date expect to hear outcome	Follow up?	Interview date	Result	Comments
Finance Officer	Care Solutions Field Lane, Northfield Middlesex NS21 3FP 01385 973073	Middlesex County Council website 09/04/10	16/04/10	✓	23/04/10		04/05/10	Unsuccessful	Second choice
Sales Account Manager	Javatec 31 Main Road, Northfield, Middlesex NS21 4XP 01385 873655	Northfield Evening News 14/04/10	21/04/10	✓	28/04/10	06/0/10 Phone call with Sarah Mackay in HR		Not shortlisted	Not enough experience
Finance Manager	APW Bridge House, School Lane, Northfield, Middlesex 01385 763967	APW website 16/04/10	17/04/10	✓	11/05/10				

Information

Directory of employment agencies	www.agencycentral.co.uk
Slivers of Time	www.sliversoftime.com
Chambers of Commerce and Industry	www.britishchambers.org.uk
Volunteering directory	www.do-it.org.uk
Jobcentre Plus	jobseekers.direct.gov.uk

The Mum's Guide to Returning to Work

Chapter Seven

CVs that employers want to see.

The beauty of writing a CV is that you are in control. You choose the structure and you put what you like on it. This means that you can design it in a way that shows you off at your best. This may mean playing down gaps in your employment, or not being forced to say why you left a job or what your salary was.

What is a CV?
- Curriculum Vitae means 'course of life' in Latin.
- That doesn't mean it should include your whole story, but it needs to be tailored to the job you are applying for.
- It is generally thought that employers take on average only 30 seconds to read a CV before making a decision on whether to shortlist you. You need to sell yourself in the first half of the first page. You are not writing an autobiography.
- It is a 'sales' document and is your opportunity to show potential employers your skills and experience. It is your chance to sell yourself to the full.

Writing a CV will remind you of your achievements and is a good way of building your confidence. Many employers (particularly in the public and voluntary sectors) prefer to use application forms, so that everyone is on an equal footing, so depending on the kind of job you are looking for, you may not need a CV. However, producing a CV, can be a useful process and a good way of getting all the information you need together in a positive way.

Content:
Personal Information:
This need only contain your name, address, phone number(s) and email address; you should not include your date of birth, nationality or marital status. You do not need to put 'Curriculum Vitae' at the top of your CV. It should be obvious what it is!

Personal Profile:
This is a more recent addition to CVs in recent years, but one which 80% of employers say that they like. A profile acts as a summary, so that the employer gets a quick picture of you, without reading the rest of the CV. Make it short and punchy and ensure the most important facts about you are here and not lost at the bottom of the

second page. The profile should say something about your background, and experience, something about your personality and a career aim which is relevant to the job you are applying for. See the example at the end of the chapter to get the picture.

Skills:
This section is not essential but it can be useful to summarise the main skills you have to offer. Keep them relevant and specific to the job you are applying for. Try not to use too many general skills or personal qualities such as 'honest', 'punctual', 'hard-working', 'good team player'. These are all good qualities to mention at some point, but will not make you stand out from the next person. Most of us can probably claim to have these qualities. Concentrate on skills which make you ideal for the job, or unique. Use the person specification to find out what the employer is looking for and emphasise these skills if you have them. Try to make sure that you give some evidence later in your CV for everything you have claimed in the personal profile and skills sections.

Employment:
- Do include voluntary work here and try to account for any gaps in a positive way. See below for how to explain gaps.
- Put your most recent job first, but if this was a short temporary job, then feel free to put your most recent relevant job and add something about temporary work at the bottom.
- Give a brief description of your role to give some background and context, but don't try to give a full job description. Emphasise anything relevant to the job you applied for. Talk about achievements and skills developed, rather than just your duties.
- You do not need to go back more than ten years if you don't think it is helpful, but if you have had a break from work and your most relevant experience was some time ago, make sure you include this. If you had a number of temporary jobs in a similar field, you may prefer to summarise these into one section.

According to recent research:
- *73% of employers had rejected candidates for short listing after finding a lack of specific achievements on their CV.* [1]
- *54% of jobseekers found it difficult to recall work based achievements.* [1]

Education:
- Again, put your most recent qualifications first.
- If you have a lot of higher level qualifications, there is no need to mention earlier qualifications such as your GCSEs.
- You do not need to mention every course you have ever been on, but you could write a sentence to summarise some of the courses you have been on, perhaps as part of your job, particularly if they are relevant.
- Put your education above your employment, if it was fairly recent or more relevant.

Other information:
You may want a section for other things you haven't covered yet, such as other skills (IT, languages, driving licence), or maybe your interests if you think they are relevant. You could also include voluntary work, groups you are involved with, professional bodies you are a member of and committees you are on.

Referees:
You do not need to include names and addresses of referees, you can put 'available on request'. However make sure you are ready to provide the name and addresses of appropriate referees when you are asked for them. See note in Chapter Eight on application forms, for more on who to use as referees.

Other points:
- Be relevant and try to leave out things which are not relevant, you do not have to say everything you have ever done. Everything you write should add to your claim that you are ideal for the job.
- Give lots of examples that provide evidence for your claims.
- Try not to use the word 'I' too much, try to write your CV as much as possible in the third person, as if someone else is describing you.
- Don't use jargon or abbreviations which the employer may not understand.
- Be prepared to rewrite your CV for each job, make sure you use the person specification if the employer has provided one and show that you have what they say they are looking for.
- Be concise - no more than two pages (there are a few exceptions to this, such as academic CVs, where it is normal to include a list of publications). Any longer and you risk the employer losing interest. If it is too long, make sure you leave out some of the jobs you did when you were younger or try to summarise them.

- Be honest and positive. Making things up will only get you into trouble – either the employer will find out that you lied, or you won't be able to admit that you are struggling with Excel when you claimed on your CV to be an expert!

Layout:
- Put your full name, in bold and centred at the head of the top sheet.
- The layout should be attractive and neat.
- Set your CV out in headed sections, with headings in capitals, bold, and/or underlined.
- Keep it to two pages maximum!
- Underline and/or bold names of schools, colleges, firms, etc., OR the names of job titles you have held, depending on the emphasis that you prefer.
- Keep it simple, use white paper and a font such as Arial or Times New Roman.
- Put your CV in an A4 envelope unfolded.
- Check and double check for spelling and grammar mistakes, don't forget to use a spell checker. Also, do get a friend or careers adviser to look it over for you, both for mistakes and to make suggestions as to how you could sell yourself better.

Help from a careers adviser made a huge difference to my feeling confident that my CV was up-to-date in its style and layout. Also, having an interview practice with her massively increased my confidence; it's hard to approach even the application process when you are sure you're out of date with how things are presented, but don't know what to change to update it.

Bridget

Remember that your CV is a personal document that reflects you and that you should feel happy with. There are no rights and wrongs with CVs, but many different ways of doing it. Choose an approach and style that suits you. By all means ask other people to help you with your CV, in particular checking for mistakes, but be careful of letting someone else write it for you (whether a friend or a professional). They will probably use words and phrases that 'are not you' and will emphasise things that you wouldn't. Let others advise and help you, but remember that you are the expert on your life, so make sure you write it!

The Mum's Guide to Returning to Work

How to explain gaps on a CV

If you've had time off work to spend with your children, the chances are that there are gaps in your career history. How do you deal with this?

Don't forget that the official date of leaving your last employment will be when your maternity leave finished, not when it started, so make sure you get this right. Bear in mind that you are not normally obliged to give exact dates of starting and leaving a job on your CV, just putting the year is usually acceptable and may hide some gaps or make them look minimal.

Look for any other gaps not explained by work or study and explain them. Employers will usually notice gaps and will usually want to know what happened. If you don't explain the gap they may assume that you have been long term sick and may not be back to full health yet; that you have been looking for a job for three years unsuccessfully, or even that you've been in prison. Far better, let them know that you have been looking after your children. However, be positive and keep to the point. The employer does not need to know how many children you have or indeed their names and ages. Simply state that you have been on a career break to raise your family. Then be positive about anything you have done and learnt during this time. The example below might help:

2005 – present:	**Career Break** Since 2005 I have been on a career break in order to spend time with my family. During this time I have attended a number of IT courses to update my skills. I have been involved in community activities, such as helping out with school fetes and setting up a babysitting circle. More recently, I have started working as a volunteer mentor for a teenager with learning disabilities. During this time I have developed skills in assertiveness, time management and budgeting.

A client of mine once admitted to me that she had lied about the dates on her CV, to cover up her career break, as she was scared that it might put employers off. We talked about how she could describe her career break in a positive way, as in the example above. She went away with a CV that was positive, honest and one that she could be proud of.

Skills based CV

So far we have talked about the most commonly used layout for a CV, the 'chronological CV'. However in some cases it may be more appropriate to consider using a 'skills based CV'. In this case, after the personal profile you would identify the most relevant skills you have to offer for the job in question. The person specification should help with this. You would then write a short paragraph on each skill, giving pertinent examples as to how you have used and developed this skill through work, voluntary work, study or home life. Next give a brief history of your working life, without going into too much detail. This style of CV is useful if you want to draw attention away from the fact that you haven't worked recently or have worked in lots of different fields. It is also useful if you are changing career and want to emphasise your transferable skills, rather than go into too many technicalities of what your previous jobs involved, where it may not be relevant.

> *Employers need to have a reason to continue reading the rest of your CV because it is their job to attract and retain the best employees for their businesses. They have little or no interest in what you want out of your career. They want to know what you will do for them, how will you benefit their business? But most CVs fall into the trap of being too self-orientated.* [2]
>
> Farhan Yasin, President of CareerBuilder EMEA

Have a look at the example on the next page for one idea of how to lay out your CV. A quick search on the internet will help you to come up with any number of other types of layouts. Choose one that you feel comfortable with.

Sarah Cowell

123 Honey Street
Townville
Wessex
S10 2HS
(01234) 567890 / 07652 12345
Sarah.cowell@ntlworld.com

Personal Profile:

> A highly competent administrator with experience in reception and customer service. Enthusiastic, hard working and efficient; good at using own initiative and a proven team-player. Now looking to consolidate experience with a challenging new role in reception work.

Skills:

- Communication – both written and verbal
- IT – proficient in a range of packages
- Customer service
- General administration
- Organisation
- Excellent telephone manner

Work Experience:

2000 – Present: **Career break and temporary work**
Since 2000 I have been on a career break in order to spend time with my family. During this time I have worked on a number of temporary administrative contracts through Jones Employment Agency. This has enabled me to keep up to date with the world of employment and required me to be a quick learner and fit quickly into a team. I have also spent time developing my IT skills and being involved in community activities, such as helping out with school fetes and setting up a babysitting circle.

1998 – 2000 **Receptionist & Administrative Assistant**; *Townville Hospital*
Responsible for greeting visitors and ensuring their needs were met, inputting patient information onto the hospital database and general filing work. This job often involved dealing with distressed or angry visitors and required me to

be sensitive, yet professional in my dealings with them. This was a busy and varied job and required excellent organisational skills and prioritisation.

1995 – 1998   **Administrative Assistant;** *Wessex County Council*
Working in a range of departments, doing general office duties, database inputting, reception work and filing. I was awarded the 'Employee of the Month' award for coming into work on a Saturday to help meet a deadline.

1993 – 1995   **Retail Assistant**; *Iceland Frozen Foods*
This was a part-time job during and after college.

Education:

2002 – 2008   **IT courses with Learndirect**:
I completed a number of distance learning courses in I.T, and achieved the European Computer Driving Licence. This included courses in Word, Excel, Access, PowerPoint, the use of Internet and email.

1993 – 1995   **BTEC National Diploma in Business Administration**
Townville Technology College
The course included modules in IT, customer service and accounts. I also did a one day a week work experience placement in a local firm of solicitors.

Other qualifications:

I have 7 GCSEs including a B in Maths and a C in English Language.

References available on request.

Cover letters

If asked to apply for a job by 'CV with cover letter', make sure you letter is as strong as your CV and well structured:
- Start by saying which job you are applying for and where you saw it advertised.
- Include a sentence as to why you are applying for the job; why the job and the company interest you. Flatter them if you can.
- Move on to say why you are an ideal candidate and explain that how you have the skills and experience they are looking for. Using the person specification, draw attention to each criterion they are looking for and give an example of how you meet this. This is very similar to filling in the 'other information' section on application forms. Have a look at Chapter Eight for more on this.
- Finish with a polite sentence saying how enthusiastic you are about the job and that you look forward to hearing from them.

Points to ponder

- Keep it short and snappy, no more than two pages.
- Use a profile as a positive introduction and summarise the key points.
- Emphasise skills and achievements, not just your job role.
- Explain any gaps and be positive about them.
- Check, check and check again.
- Keep it relevant to the job, you don't have to include everything.
- Finally, be positive and don't forget to blow your own trumpet – it is expected in a CV.

Reading

Max Eggert, *Perfect CV,* Random House Books, 2007

Jim Bright & Joanne Earl, *Brilliant CV: What Employers Want to See and How to Say it,* Prentice Hall, 2007

The Mum's Guide to Returning to Work

Chapter Eight

Application Forms –
How to Secure an Interview

What is it for?

So you've written your fabulous CV, but the employer you've seen an advert for wants applicants to complete one of their standard application forms, rather than to send a CV. This can be frustrating, but don't despair. Producing your CV has helped you to distil the key facts about yourself and to identify your main skills. You've probably come up with some great little positive phrases you can use again, and all the dates you need are at your fingertips.

Employers use application forms to compare and contrast applicants easily. They will use them to prepare a shortlist of, say, six to eight candidates to invite for interview. Your task is to get yourself an interview. Give it the time it deserves to do the application justice and don't rush it. If necessary concentrate on completing a few applications well, rather than lots badly.

As a very general rule of thumb, you are more likely to be asked to apply for a job with an application form in the public and voluntary sector and with a CV in the private sector. However, this is not always the case, so be prepared for either approach.

At first, application forms can feel fairly straightforward. You have a structure and the questions tend to be fairly straightforward and factual at the beginning; that is until you get to the dreaded 'other information' section which is where most of us get stuck. Application forms can also be tricky to complete because they can make little allowance for anyone who hasn't followed a run-of-the-mill career route. You may be wondering:

- What do you do when your most recent job isn't your most relevant one?
- Where do you put a career break?
- Who do I put down as referees?
- And of course - how do you complete the tricky 'other information' section?

We will come to all of these issues in turn, but first let's start with some general tips on filling in application forms:

The Basics

- Do your research. Find out as much as you can about the organisation, the role and the field or sector in general.
- Read through any accompanying documents, including the job description and person specification and guidelines for completing the form, if provided.
- Word process the form if you can. Gone are the days when forms had to be hand written so that employers could see what your hand writing was like. Ask the employer to email the form to you if necessary, or at least word process the 'other information' section and complete the rest in pen as neatly as possible. Increasingly applications can be filled in online now.
- Make sure your spelling and grammar are accurate – use a spellchecker and ask a friend to check for you as well.
- Ensure you explain your previous jobs carefully; as with CVs, don't assume that the employer will understand your previous roles or any jargon or acronyms you have used.
- Answer all the questions, even if they don't seem relevant - they are all there for a reason.
- Be honest but make as many positive statements about yourself as you can - you are trying to sell yourself.
- Keep a copy of your completed form; don't forget to print it out if it is an online application. Also keep a copy of the original advertisement, job description and person specification if you have them.
- You could enclose a short covering letter with the form highlighting any points that are especially relevant, including where you saw the advertisement or the reference number. However, if you are not specifically asked to include a letter be aware that the employers may only look at the application form, so do not include anything in a letter that is not already on the form.
- Don't include your CV, if it's not been asked for.

My most recent job isn't my most relevant one

In designing application forms, employers tend to assume that the applicant has had a fairly standard career progression and they don't tend to make concessions for someone who doesn't fit the mould. Often a form will ask for detailed information about your current or most recent job and will only ask for the bare facts of any other jobs.

If perhaps you've been doing a bit of temping or a supermarket job that fits in with school hours and are now looking to go back to something more challenging, you are probably not going to be selling yourself by going into detail about what you are doing at the moment. I suggest that you describe your most recent *relevant* job, as this is what will sell you to the employer and in reality is what they really need to know about.

You will need to add a note to explain why you have done this and ensure you include your current job somewhere on the form. There is the risk that you will lose favour for not following the employer's instructions to the letter, but you will sell yourself better by doing this.

How do I describe my career break?

Make sure you include it. It is not strictly speaking your 'most recent job', but it is worth describing somewhere, perhaps in the 'other jobs' section. Have a look at the previous chapter on application forms for advice on how to describe your career break. As with application forms, explain what you have done and be positive about it.

Who do I put down as referees?

This can be a tricky one if you've not worked recently, especially if employers are asking for the name of your current or most recent employer. Do follow the employer's instructions as far as possible but consider the following points:

- If you are still in contact with your previous employer and happy to seek them out, do use them, even if it was some time ago. Whatever they can say about your work five years ago should still be relevant - you won't have changed that much!
- If your previous boss has moved to another organisation and you can track them down, do still use them as long as you explain how you know them.
- If you have done any courses recently, you could ask your

tutor to act as a referee. They may not be able to comment on your ability in a work situation, but they could make comments such as, for example: about your punctuality, making contact when you are likely to be absent, that you contribute in a respectful and constructive way in discussions, that you have good academic insight, hand all your assignments in on time, or that you support other students who are struggling.

- Unless an employer specifically says not to, it is usually appropriate to use a supervisor from a voluntary work placement as a referee. As always, make sure you ask permission for giving someone's name as a referee.
- Generally references from friends are not acceptable unless you are really desperate or unless they can talk about you in another context, such as being members of a committee together.
- If you still can't think of anyone you could use, now might be a good time to start establishing your credentials for a reference by doing some voluntary work, trying to find some temporary work or starting a course.

How do I complete the 'other information' section?

This is usually the bit which most of us complete last and then dither over for ages, not being sure quite where to start. Sound familiar? It is easy to think that we don't have anything else very relevant to add and tempting just to leave it blank in the hope that the employer will be so impressed by our previous work experience that they will just shortlist us anyway. Please don't do this, as it really is the most important section of the form, where you have the chance to convince the employer that you have exactly what they are looking for.

Don't let it become a page full of vague waffle about your career path, your personal experiences and your views on pertinent matters. The employer won't be interested and probably won't read on to the end.

This section doesn't have to be as hard as you might think and can actually be quite straightforward if you do it right. Start by looking at the person specification. The employer will have spent time thinking about their ideal candidate, and will hopefully have written a person specification to detail exactly what types of skills, qualifications, experiences and knowledge they are looking for. They may say whether each of these criteria is desirable or essential. If they are being really helpful they will tell you whether they are looking for these criteria at the application stage, at the interview or through a test.

Use this information to your advantage and use this space to explain why you are the person they have envisaged when writing the person specification. Imagine that the employer has a chart in front of them, listing all the criterion on the person specification down one side and the names of candidates along the top. They will be looking to put a tick or a score out of ten against each criterion for each candidate and will be looking through the form to see how each candidate measures up to each criterion. You therefore need to make it easy for them, by listing each criterion in order and giving a short sentence explaining why you believe you meet it and giving relevant examples to demonstrate it. Not all employers are as structured in their approach to short listing, but assume they do it this way and you will produce a well structured application.

So start off with a short paragraph explaining why you are applying for the job, why it interests you and why you want to work for this particular organisation. Flatter them if you can!

Then move on to explain why you think you are the ideal candidate and list each of the points on the person specification in turn. Put a heading for each one, perhaps in bold and don't be afraid to use the same words or phrases used by the employer. Some people feel this is cheating, but when you look at it from their point of view, it makes it so much easier to find the information they are looking for.

Let's say an employer is looking for someone with skills in public speaking. In the waffle approach you may mention at some point that you have given a talk to groups of clients about your company's research and perhaps at a later stage say that you have given talks to a class of children about your knowledge of living in Africa. The employer may deduce from this that you have skills in public speaking, but if they have to scan through your form for each criterion they are looking for, this may not stand out strongly. Far better to put something like this:

> **Public Speaking:** I enjoy public speaking and feel that this is a skill which I have developed well over the years. I have experience of speaking to a range of client groups of different sizes and on different topics. For example, when working for ARP I would regularly give talks at business conferences to groups of 100 delegates or more about the research project I had been working on. I have also been invited by my daughter's school to give a talk to a group of 30 eight year olds about my experience of living and working in Africa.

Make it as easy as possible for the employer to see that you have what they are looking for. Spell it out to them in the order you know they want and forget the life story. Remember they may have a hundred or more applications to look at. Make yours easy to read and you are far more likely to make it to the shortlist pile than the reject pile.

Use lots of relevant and varied examples as evidence of the qualities and skills you claim to have and try to emphasise achievements and things you have done which are 'beyond the call of duty', rather than just duties that are required of you.

Conclude with a really positive statement about how much you feel you can bring to the job and how much it interests you.

Points to ponder

- Be honest, relevant and positive – sell yourself!
- Show how you used your career break to develop yourself and your skills.
- Address each criterion in the person specification and give relevant examples to demonstrate you fit it.
- Find appropriate referees.
- Do your research about the job and the company.
- Follow the instructions and complete each section.
- Take your time and check and double check for mistakes.

Reading

Rebecca Corfield, *Career Success: Preparing the Perfect Job Application: Application Forms and Letters Made Easy: 4,* Kogan Page, 2009

Chapter Nine

Succeeding at interview

So you've been invited for an interview, you've managed to jump the first hurdle. Well done! You've shown on paper that you are up to the job, now you need to prove this in person and show that you are better than the other candidates. I often feel that interviews are a cruel and unfair way of selecting people for a job. Many people get nervous and don't perform well in an interview situation, when they may well be ideal for a job, but just can't prove that to an employer. Whether or not this applies to you, I hope the following tips will help you.

Preparation:
- Make sure you contact the employer to tell them that you can attend the interview and let them know if you have any special requirements.
- Find out as much as you can about the company and the department, project or team you are going to be involved with. Read any information they have sent you, look at their website and ask family or friends who may know something about them.
- Find out about any changes in government policy and new developments in the sector which might affect the work you would be doing.
- Look at your application and remind yourself why you applied for the job and why you think you would be a good candidate.
- Think about the kinds of questions you are likely to be asked (see below) and practice answering them. Thorough preparation here is essential and will make a huge difference.
- Make sure you know how to get to the interview and leave plenty of time.
- Think carefully about what you are going to wear and try on your outfit the day before. As a guide, dress smartly, but this does not always mean wearing a suit - plain neutral colours and simple accessories are best. Make sure you feel comfortable.
- Ensure you have childcare in place and perhaps a back up plan in case one of the children is ill.

- Plan the questions you are going to ask. Write them down; you may choose to take them with you.

What will the interview be like?

You should have been told whether you will have to do any tests or are required to do a presentation or take part in a group activity. If you are not sure what any of this will involve, make sure you contact the employer to find out more.

Interviews will tend to take on one of two formats. The first one is the more traditional approach where the employer will ask questions related to your application such 'tell me why you moved from retail management to marketing' or 'tell me about the project you managed for PLC and what you feel you achieved from this'. They will ask each candidate different questions tailored to their experience and are likely to probe you and ask follow up questions if they want to know more. To prepare for this kind of interview make sure you look carefully at your application and are prepared to answer questions about any gaps, career moves or anything else they might be interested in.

This kind of interview will feel like a conversation and very much a two way process, where you feel the employer is interested in you as an individual and you will tend to get a good feel for how you are getting on.

The alternative is a more structured 'competency based' interview where each candidate is asked exactly the same question. They may not ask lots of follow-up or probing questions, so make sure you give full answers. Increasingly employers are moving towards this more structured approach to ensure that they are not discriminating against the candidates by asking different questions. Questions will be along the lines of 'Can you give an example of when you have had to face a difficult customer and how you dealt with them'? Or they may be based on a scenario: 'What would you do in a situation where you had three deadlines to meet and the phone keeps ringing?' Or they could be more general such as: 'Tell us about your IT skills', or 'Do you have any experience of setting up a website'?

If you know what kind of interview you are likely to get, it makes it easier to prepare for. Within the public sector; local government, civil service, NHS, schools, charities you are probably more likely to get the competency based interview as they will be keen to follow equal opportunities guidelines. In the private sector you may get a more traditional approach or perhaps a combination of the two.

How to guess interview questions

The purpose of the interview is for the employer to find out if you are the ideal candidate. They have already described their 'ideal candidate' in the person specification and they will use this to find out who best matches this profile. In all likelihood (particularly in the competency approach described above) they will ask questions relating to each of the skills, knowledge and experiences they have listed on the person specification and they will then give a score or tick against each criterion and, theoretically, offer the job to the candidate with the highest overall score.

So if for example the person specification states that they are looking for someone who can use their initiative, a question might be: 'Can you give an example of when you have used your initiative in a work situation?' or they may give you a scenario to test if you can use your initiative like: 'If you arrived at work one day and found that your line manager was on holiday and the receptionist was off sick, what would you do?'

Use the person specification to have a go at guessing interview questions, prepare some answers to them and practice answering them. Beware of preparing so much that you answer in a robot-like fashion and ensure you answer the question they asked, which may not necessarily be exactly the same as the one you prepared for! At least make sure you have thought of a good example you could mention for everything listed on the person specification.

Remember, if you have a more traditional unstructured type of interview (as described above) you will also get questions related to your own situation, so be prepared for these too.

Here are some examples of possible questions:

General questions:
- Tell us why you have applied for this job
- What skills do you have that make you an ideal candidate?
- What are your strengths/weaknesses?

Personal questions:
- What did you learn on your course?
- Why did you take a career break?
- Tell us more about the project you have just finished working on.
- Why did you move from engineering to architecture?

Examples:
Can you give us an example of when you have had to:
- Deal with a difficult customer?
- Delegate tasks to get a job done?
- Use your organisational skills?

Scenarios:
What would you do if:
- A customer was abusive or aggressive to you?
- You realised that you had made a mistake on an invoice you had sent out?
- Someone rang up asking for the home phone number of one your clients?

Knowledge:
- Why do you think confidentiality is important in this role?
- What do you understand the purpose of this role to be?
- What recent changes in government legislation will you need to be aware of in this role?

Experience:
What experience do you have of:
- Working with children with special needs?
- Working in the health care sector?
- Working in an unsupervised role?

Questions in the last four categories will be easy to guess from the person specification.

At the interview

- It is important to be on time. Arrive ten minutes early and if you are delayed for any reason telephone the employer to let them know.
- First impressions count. Be polite to everyone you meet; someone showing you round may be asked for their opinion of you.
- Switch off your mobile phone (obvious I know!).
- If you are offered a drink think carefully before you accept it. It can be distracting to talk and drink at the same time.
- Be honest and positive, admit if you don't know the answer to a question or don't have much experience of something, but show that you are keen and willing to learn.
- Try to use every question to show yourself in the best light possible.
- Give examples wherever possible to illustrate a point.
- Think carefully before answering; think about the main points you want to make and then carefully go through each one.
- Don't be critical of former bosses, colleagues or companies.
- Make sure you listen carefully to the question and give a relevant answer, keep to the point and don't just waffle about the subject generally.
- Keep your answers short and relevant - between 30 seconds and two minutes – and simple and clear. Look at the interviewer's body language to judge whether or not you have said enough. Speak as you would normally.
- Don't assume the interviewer knows what you are talking about and that they can remember what you wrote on your application.
- Sit comfortably well back in your chair, cross your legs, if that is comfortable for you. You may want to hold your hands in your lap to stop yourself fiddling with your hands.
- Keep good eye contact. In a panel interview, always address your answer to the person who asked the question, but glance at the others if they are looking, to show that you are acknowledging them.

The first interview was nerve wracking. If you get an interview, before you go along, do as much research as you can and dress properly for the interview. I've seen some people dress casually and others dress as if they are going to a funeral. Don't give up; there is a job there for you somewhere.

Deborah

How to deal with difficult situations

You go blank and don't know how to answer a question:
This often happens and good interviewers are usually prepared for this and will be sympathetic. Explain that you are nervous and that your mind has gone blank; ask politely if you can return to the question at the end. Hopefully by the end you will feel more relaxed and more able to answer the question.

You can't think of any relevant examples:
As above, you could ask to come back to it, but you may just not have a relevant one to give, in which case give them a made up scenario, eg:

'I can't actually think of an example of when a customer has been aggressive towards me, but if that did happen, I would stay calm, listen to their point of view and try to be helpful. If necessary I would make it clear that I was not prepared to listen to abusive language and if the customer did not leave or calm down I would call for my line manager to come and help, and be prepared to press an alarm button if necessary.'

Obviously if you have prepared well, you may have anticipated this question and have prepared a good example!

You don't understand a question:
Politely ask if they would mind rephrasing the question or ask them to explain the meaning of certain words.

You are asked about your children or childcare arrangements:
This could be considered sexual discrimination as it is unlikely that a man would be asked similar questions. It would be perfectly reasonable to refuse to answer such a question and to follow this up with the Equality and Human Rights Commission[1], however you may prefer to give a short answer such as: 'As I'm sure you would find with any working mother or father, I will ensure that I have child care in place and back up plans should I need it.'

After the interview

Whilst the interview is still fresh in your mind, jot down some thoughts on what went well and what you need to improve on. Make a note of questions you found hard to answer and think through how you could improve on similar ones in the future. Now you just need to play a waiting game. With any luck the employer will soon be in touch to tell you that they would like to offer you a job. In which case move onto the next chapters in the book for advice on what to do next. If however you are unsuccessful (and you can't expect to succeed every time), don't lose heart. Try to be positive and think about what you have learnt from the experience. It is perfectly reasonable to ask the employer to give you some feedback as to why you weren't successful this time. They may be willing to give you some useful advice as to how you came across at interview and how you could come across better next time.

Don't give yourself a hard time, if at first you are not successful with an application or interview, see it as an experience and seek feedback from the interview.

Anita

Most importantly, keep trying and don't give up!

Points to ponder

- Preparation is key. Find out about the role and the organisation.
- Guess some questions and practice answering them.
- Take your time if you get a tricky question.
- Be positive, friendly and let your personality shine through.
- Don't forget your body language.
- Don't let nerves get the better of you, just do your best and if nothing else think of it as good practice.

Reading

James Innes, *The Interview Book: Your Definitive Guide to the Perfect Interview Technique,* Prentice Hall, 2009

Chapter Ten

Flexible Working – Making it Work for You

Your plan may be to go back to work full-time. This could be through choice, financial necessity or because you don't feel that your particular field is suited to part-time work. Finding a full-time job is generally more straightforward than finding a part-time one, but childcare may be a major issue for you. For many women however, part-time working or flexible working (if it can be found) seems the best way to combine work and motherhood. It is not easy though; so many of the women I speak to are frustrated by not being able to find a job in hours to suit them:

According to the Netmums website survey 'The Great Work Debate' in 2005: *'18% of mums working full-time would 'prefer to work part time but can't find a suitable job'*, while 21% of mums who stay at home said: *'I would rather work but can't find a job that offers the hours/flexibility I would need'*[1]

While finding flexible work is not easy, the situation is improving. In 2003 the government introduced the right to request flexible working to employees with children (now) under sixteen. Employers are starting to become more open to the idea of flexible working and can see the benefits in it for both them and their employees. However there is still a long way to go. The right to request flexible working is only open to employees who have been with their employer for 26 weeks or more and is not open to new employees, therefore not something that a woman returner (who has left their previous employment) has a legal right to ask for.

Later we'll have a look at how to find a flexible job or to negotiate flexible hours, but first let's look at what we mean by flexible working and what options are available.

Types of flexible working

Flexible working can come in many forms, the most common ones being listed below. It could involve combining a number of these options, for example working term-time, 20 hours per week and including one day working from home.

Part time working
Part time working simply means working fewer hours than the standard working week. This could mean working two or three full days or perhaps four or five shorter days. Legally employers are obliged to not treat part-time workers less favourably than full-time workers.

Flexi-time
Flexi-time allows you to vary your hours, although there may be 'core' time where you have to work and an expected number of working hours a day. You may have the option to cover your hours over fewer days per week. You may also be able to take time off in lieu (TOIL) for extra hours you have worked, perhaps saving up time to take off in the school holidays.

Job sharing
Job sharing is where one job role is split, usually between two (or sometimes more) people. For example one person might do mornings and another afternoons, or one could do Mondays and Tuesdays and the other Wednesdays, Thursdays and Fridays. Sometimes there is a period when both job sharers are in the office to liaise and handover. This is increasingly common in positions where it is essential for one person to be there at all times, for example teachers, managers or receptionists.

Term-Time working
This allows you to work full or part-time during the school term only, while taking unpaid leave in the holidays. Your pay may be averaged out over the year.

Compressed hours
You work more hours a day but fewer days a week.

V-Time
This means a voluntary reduction in hours, maybe for an agreed period of time. This could include the chance to 'flex-up' or 'flex-down' your holidays for more or less pay.

Working from home
Also called teleworking or remote working. You could work all or part of the week at home. Working from home should not be seen as a substitute for childcare for young children, although it can still

be useful as it cuts down on commuting time. Your employer is still responsible for your health and safety when working at home, so can insist that you have the correct equipment and childcare in place.

So what working pattern would be right for you?

Clearly if you have a very rigid idea of what hours you are prepared to work, you are going to find it hard to find a suitable job. Employers have got a long way to go in offering more flexible working options for staff, but try to be flexible yourself and meet them halfway, as you are far more likely to be successful if you do. What are the ideal hours you would like to work? Obviously the fewer hours you work, the less you will earn. Now have a think about the maximum number of hours you would be prepared to work. Remember employers don't have to offer you a job. If you insist that the only job you will take is one between the hours of 10am and 2pm on Tuesdays and Wednesdays during term time, you may be waiting a long time! Try to be flexible and think about all the options; bearing some of the following in mind:

- If your children are school age, could they go to after-school club on one or more days a week and a holiday club for some of the school holidays?
- If you have a partner who is working, what could they do to help? They may have the right to request flexible working even if you don't.
- Could you fit in more hours if you started work early and your partner finished late?
- Could your partner finish work early one afternoon a week to collect the children from school?
- Don't forget that you and your partner will both have annual leave to help cover school holidays, but do make sure you leave some overlap to go away as a family!
- Are there grandparents or other family members or friends who would like to look after the children one day a week, or for a few days in the holidays?
- Could you leave work earlier if you took a shorter lunch break?
- Could you work from home one day a week to reduce travelling time, or make up a few hours in the evenings?

By finding a way to squeeze in a few more hours than you had perhaps envisaged, you might realise that you could consider more jobs than you thought. If you are paying for after-school childcare, working those few extra hours in the afternoons may not be worth it to you financially, but it might just make the difference for your employer and secure you the job you want.

How to find a job that is not full-time

Work for yourself
In Chapter Five we looked at options for setting up a business, working from home and doing freelance work. In theory any of these ideas would allow you to work the hours you want, but it may not be that straightforward. Setting up your own business can take over your life – finishing work at 3pm or 5pm may not be an option if you want your business to survive. As a freelancer, saying 'no' to a client who is pressing you for a deadline could lose you the contract.

Share the load
More fathers than ever before are working flexible hours in order to share child care responsibilities with their partners. I know a consultant and head of a hospital department, a legal adviser for a major national charity and the marketing manager for a building society, all men, who work flexible hours to fit in with family life. However, in the majority of cases, the responsibility for finding childcare and taking on more flexible hours to suit the family is still the woman's. Does it have to be this way? Perhaps you could be creative about how you work things out together? Is your partner's career really more important than yours? For some lone parents, shared custody may free you up to work part of the week, but for others this won't be an option.

Find a job that's advertised as part-time
Employers are starting to wake up to the fact that there is a huge untapped pool of skilled workers out there, just waiting for a part-time opportunity to arise. More and more often jobs are advertised as part-time or as a job-share and increasingly employers say that they will consider flexible options. Clearly these are the jobs to apply for, but bear in mind that part-time jobs tend to be popular and there may well be fierce competition for them.

Have a look at the websites www.workingmums.co.uk and www.jobs4mothers.com which advertise jobs with flexible working options; they also include lots of opportunities in self-employment and homeworking. Every year www.timesonline.co.uk publishes a list of the top fifty places where women want to work, or similarly www.wherewomenwanttowork.com publishes a free downloadable guide annually.

Generally jobs related to education, particularly in schools (and sometimes further education colleges or universities) lend themselves to working school hours. Apart from the obvious ones such as teachers and teaching assistants, options include working as a finance manager, school secretary, librarian, counsellor, careers adviser, family therapist, home school liaison worker, educational psychologist or speech therapist among others. Not all of these posts would be employed directly by the school or necessarily fit exactly into school hours (nor may you be qualified to do them!), but they might give you some ideas.

Consider downgrading
I hesitate to suggest this, because it shouldn't have to be necessary, but it is a fact that part-time workers are more likely to be in less skilled jobs than full-time workers. There is a perception among some employers that part-time work is not feasible in higher level or management jobs. It is a painful fact that by downgrading your ideas and applying for a lower skilled job than you are used to, you may be more likely to find part-time work. However, looking on the positive side, maybe doing a less demanding job would be just what you need for your return to the workplace initially. Less stress may make your return smoother and doing a less challenging job for while could be a real boost to your confidence. Within six months you may be doing so well that you are promoted to a better position, and you may then be able to negotiate that role to be part-time.

Hidden jobs
As mentioned in Chapter Six, 80% of jobs are never advertised. If you are making a speculative approach to employers, say that you are looking for part-time hours. You will cost less than a full-time employee and they may be more willing to create a new position for you. They may have just had a current member of staff go off on maternity leave or come back part-time and could really do with someone to fill in for one or two days a week. Networking will be essential in order to identify such opportunities.

Full-time jobs
Don't assume that a job advertised as 'full-time' has to be full-time. Try asking an employer if they would take you on a part-time basis,

thus saving them money, or to take on two members of staff on a job-share basis and get twice the skills and experience. It is easy for employers to just assume that any given role needs to take 37.5 hours per week. If a company decides that they need to take on a new member of staff to be responsible for their marketing, does it need to be a full-time role? Maybe 20 hours work a week would be enough to get the job done. Anyone who works part-time will tell you that part-time workers are often (although I'm sure not always) far more efficient than full-timers.

When applying for a new position, as a new employee you don't have the right to request flexible working, but that doesn't mean you can't ask even if the job is advertised as full-time. The tricky part is knowing when to ask the employer for flexible hours. You could apply for the job and go through the whole application and interview process and raise the issue when (if) you are offered the job. From a legal point of view, this might be best, as for an employer to turn down a request for flexible working at this point could be construed as indirect sexual discrimination. You also have the advantage that by this point they are convinced that you are the best person for the job and may be willing to bend over backwards to keep you. On the other hand you could be seen as being underhand and dishonest for not raising the issue sooner, and this may not be the best start with a new employer.

Alternatively you could ask at an earlier stage. How about ringing up an employer for a chat when you see a job advert that interests you. Find out if they would consider offering any flexible working options. If they say no, you have lost nothing, but if they are positive, you know you can go ahead with your application having been honest from the start and knowing that they will take any requests from you seriously. Raising the issue at interview is another option, enabling you to convince an employer of your strengths first, but being honest about what you want before an offer is made.

There are pros and cons with each approach and not really a 'right' answer to this issue. I think it depends on how family-friendly the employer is, how part-time you want to work and whether you would be prepared to work full-time if your request wasn't granted. Don't forget that if you do end up having to work full-time initially, after six months you will have the right to request flexible working. Use that time to convince your employer that you are invaluable and they will be more likely to do what they can to keep you.

The Mum's Guide to Returning to Work

Pauline responded to an advert for a job as an admin assistant for a small property company. Although the job was advertised as full-time, before applying she rang the employer to ask whether he would consider taking on a part-time secretary. He said he was very open to the idea and suggested she apply. Pauline was offered the job and then they discussed hours. He was willing to offer her four short (school hours) days a week, term-time only, which she gratefully accepted. He realised that this was more than enough hours to get the job done; the answer machine would take messages when Pauline wasn't there and he saved more than 50% on his admin costs!

Denise applied for a job as a support worker with a housing trust. She put in a good application, was short listed and at the interview asked if they would consider taking her on part-time. The employer explained that they were an equal opportunities employer and were happy to try to accommodate employees. She was offered the job and then discussed hours with them. By this stage the interview panel were so impressed by her that they were pretty much willing to take her on whatever terms she asked for. They said yes to three and a half days a week, so she tried her luck in asking for four weeks of extra unpaid leave per year to help her cover the school holidays. Again got a positive response!

Points to ponder

- Consider carefully how many hours and what pattern you are prepared to work. The more flexible you can be the more chance you have of finding something.
- Don't be scared to ask an employer to make a full-time job part-time.
- Share the load with your partner if you can.

Information

Websites advertising part-time jobs aimed at mums	www.workingmums.co.uk www.jobs4mothers.com
List of top 50 places where women want to work	www.timesonline.co.uk

Downloadable guide of "women friendly" employers	www.wherewomenwanttowork.com
Information on different flexible working options and advice on negotiating flexible working	www.workingfamilies.org.uk
A list of family friendly employers	www.topemployersforworkingfamilies.org

Chapter Eleven

Childcare

Finding childcare you are happy with will make all the difference to you feeling happy about going off to work and being able to concentrate on work when you get there. Most of us will need to consider childcare options when we go back to work, unless: our partner is at home to look after the children (an increasingly likely option), the children are old enough to look after themselves, or you are lucky enough to find a job that fits exactly into school hours and terms. If you've been lucky enough to achieve one of the above options, then you can skip to the next chapter!

There has been lots of research and debate in the press as to the benefits or otherwise of children in childcare settings. The results are fairly inconclusive, but some points you might want to bear in mind are:

- Babies need lots of cuddles and one to one attention and they also need to be able to bond with individual carers.
- All children need to be stimulated, talked to, entertained and kept safe.
- A happy mum leads to a happy child. If you are miserable at home, your child will not be in the most positive environment. Would your child be better off with quality time, rather than quantity, although will you actually be able to provide quality time at the end of a busy day?
- Guilt is an extremely unproductive emotion. Stop worrying about what other people think and make a decision about work hours and childcare that you know is right for your children.
- Why does it have to be the women (usually) who take responsibility for childcare? If you have a partner, can they share the load in making a decision about childcare and share the dropping off or collecting?
- If you are not happy with the idea of full-time or even any childcare for your child, but want or need to go back to work, could your partner work flexibly to accommodate this? Does it always need to be the woman who works part-time?

My two children have at different times been cared for by a childminder, a private nursery, a state nursery school, a playgroup, a workplace crèche, an after-school club and holiday clubs, as well as occasional fill-in help from friends and family members. Choosing childcare is a personal thing and you will have your own views as to what is right for your family. In this chapter we look at the different types of childcare available, how to secure the childcare you need and what to do when it all goes wrong.

What types of childcare are there: pros and cons of each

Pre-school children

For a pre-school child, your primary concern will be that they are safe, secure, happy and well cared for in a warm, friendly environment. Who is looking after them may well be more important to you than where they are looked after. You will also want to ensure that your child is learning and developing in an appropriate way for their age. There are a number of options to consider and your choice will depend on how much you can afford and your personal preferences as to what you feel will be right for your child.

1.   Nanny

A nanny looks after your child in your own home. They do not have to be qualified or registered to work in your home, although nannies can now join a voluntary 'General Childcare Register' if they fulfil certain requirements.

Pros:
- Will look after your child when ill.
- Flexible hours, negotiated by you.
- You do not need to get your child out of the house in the morning as the nanny comes to you.
- If you want your child to go to the park every day, or to go to a particular baby music class or swimming lesson, you can within reason ask the nanny to do that.
- The nanny may by agreement, be responsible for cooking your child's meals and washing their clothes.
- With negotiation your nanny may be able to do some extra jobs for you such as babysitting in the evening, or some cleaning.

Cons:
- You may not like someone else working in your home.
- If your nanny is sick, you will need to find emergency cover.
- It is an expensive option, but if you have more than one child, or use a nanny share, it may work out cheaper than a nursery or child minder.
- Nanny shares can work very well, but you need to have agreement with the other parents on a number of issues and be prepared for the other family to pull out of the arrangement, if for example they were to have another child, or to move to a new area.
- You are the employer and need to be prepared to take on the responsibilities required by this, such as paying the salary, tax and national insurance. You are legally obliged to provide a work contract.

How to find a nanny

You may employ anyone you like, however it may well be sensible to use a nanny agency to help you find a nanny with suitable qualifications and experience. They will check references, conduct interviews and will be able to advise on the legal side of things, as well as how to arrange tax and National Insurance payments. They may also be able to provide cover in the event of your nanny being sick, or to help set up a nanny share arrangement for you. www.nannyjob.co.uk will help you find agencies in your area, or try asking for a recommendation of an agency from friends who have a nanny.

2.   Childminders

Childminders care for children in their own home, as opposed to working in a nursery or in the child's own home. They have strict regulations as to the number of children of different ages that they are allowed to care for and they have to be registered with and inspected by OfSted. Childminders are not required to have childcare qualifications (other than a first aid certificate), although many do. They often have their own children and may have lots of experience of caring for children.

Pros:
- Many childminders will drop-off or collect from a local school, so you may be able to continue using them when your child starts school.
- Your child will be cared for in a home environment, probably with other children to socialise with.

- Your child will get to do 'normal' everyday things, such as going to the shops, park or toddler groups.
- Your child will get to bond with one adult, who will hopefully become special to them.

Cons:
- Childminders may have their own routines which your child will need to fit in with, such as collecting older children from school.
- As with nannies, there are no other adults around, so you have to trust your childminder to provide adequate care when you are not there.
- They will probably not be able to look after your child if the child is ill. You may also need to find emergency cover if your childminder is ill.
- Childminders may not offer such long hours as nurseries or nannies, and some do not work in school holidays.

How to find a childminder

A recommendation from local parents is usually the best way. Go to toddler groups in your area and ask around, as you may well meet childminders at toddler groups and can quietly observe them. Every local authority is obliged to provide a 'Families Information Service' which provides details of local registered childcare, including childminders. Go to www.familyinformationservices.org.uk to find your local one. You will need to visit several childminders to find one you are happy with. Ask the childminder if you can contact other parents to ask their views. My daughter's first childcare was from a wonderful childminder who came to me by recommendation. She loved being with children and I could tell straight away that my daughter would be well cared for. So I was really disappointed when she decided to give up childminding and this was one factor in me choosing to give up work after having my second child.

3.   Nurseries

Day nurseries will normally open on all week days throughout the year ie not term time only. Opening hours will tend to be from around 7am or 8am in the morning through to 6pm or 7pm in the evening. They are for children from birth to school age and provide care and learning activities in different age groups.

Nursery schools are often linked to a primary school or children's centres and will be open in term time from around 9am to 3.30pm. They are usually for three to five year olds and children will often attend for just half a day at a time, which will often be free (see below). They may offer some wrap-around childcare for an extra cost.

Private nursery schools will offer a similar service, but often with more flexible hours. All three and four year olds are entitled to 15 hours of free early education for 38 weeks of the year. This entitlement may be used with some but not all private and state nursery schools, day nurseries, playgroups and with registered childminders.

Pros:
- Your child is looked after by a number of different carers, which makes some parents feel safer.
- Your child has the chance to mix with other children and take part in a variety of educational activities.
- The nursery will stay open even if a member of staff is off sick.
- Some nurseries will be very flexible with hours; others may not offer part-time places.
- Nurseries will normally have a planned and structured programme of activities.

Cons:
- Some people feel that nurseries offer too institutional an environment for young children.
- You may have little choice in the activities your child is involved with.
- Your child will probably be cared for by a number of different adults, although they may have a key worker who has particular responsibility for caring for your child.
- Your child will not have the chance to do some of the everyday things they may do at home, such as going to the park or shops.
- Nursery schools may not operate in hours to fit in with your work, though nursery schools may offer 'wraparound' care before or after sessions or you may need to find a childminder to fill the gaps.

4.   Au Pairs

An au pair will usually be a young person from a European Union country who has come to the UK to study English. They will provide an agreed number of childcare hours per week, in return for board, lodging and pocket money. This can work well if you only need a few hours of help per week, have the space and are happy to have someone living with you as part of your family. It is a cheap option, but not for everyone. The International Au Pair Association www.iapa.org will be able to provide you with details of agencies in your area that can provide all the information you need about au pairs and help to match you with someone suitable.

5. Family

If you have a partner, look at the options for you both working flexibly and sharing the childcare to maximise the hours available. Some people are lucky enough to have parents around who can help with childcare. This can be an excellent option, knowing that your children are with someone who really cares for them. However, there can be pitfalls:

- Make sure that by caring for your children, your relationship with your parents/in-laws doesn't suffer.
- Don't take them for granted and assume they will care for your children full-time till they start school. Often an arrangement of one day a week can work well.
- Your parents/in-laws may want to go on holiday or have other occasional commitments which could leave you in the lurch
- Do you share views and values on child rearing? What if your mum lets the children sit in front of the TV all day eating sweets, if that is not what you would want for them?
- You could pay your parents/in-laws to look after your children, so that it is on a more formal basis, but you may not be able to claim help with childcare costs for this arrangement (see next chapter for more on this).

School age children

Once your child reaches school age, you may be forgiven for thinking that childcare suddenly gets easier. Think again. This is actually when it gets more complicated and is frequently a time when mums choose to give up work, rather than go back to work. With a pre-schooler, you basically need to find childcare that covers all the hours you work, whatever that may be. Once your child starts school, you have some free childcare in place, but will most likely have to find other care to cover the hours outside of school time. You may be lucky enough to find work to fit within the school day, (including your travelling time) and within school term only, but these jobs are few and far between and more often than not lower paid and lower skilled. As we saw in the previous chapter holding out for a job that fits these hours will seriously limit your options, so you may have to agree to work some long days and school holidays to get the job you want, even if it is only two or three days a week.

The school day usually runs from around 9am to 3.30pm, so you may need to find cover before and after school, as well as the school holidays. Add to that teacher training days and unexpected days off for things such as snow and you can see the challenge.

6.   After school and breakfast clubs

State funded primary schools are now required to provide an 'Extended Schools' service. A fully extended school will provide childcare and activities from 8am to 6pm 48 weeks of the year. This may be in the form of breakfast clubs, after school clubs and holiday clubs. Normally these clubs will be on the school premises, or nearby with a drop-off/collection service provided. Children will be offered snacks and will have a range of activities to be involved in. There will be a charge for these clubs and you will need to book in advance. Sometimes there can be a high demand for places, so book a place as soon as you can.

Most schools will also have a range of after school activities, such as sports clubs, music groups, gardening, chess or craft clubs which may also extend the childcare day for you. These kinds of activities may not always be a reliable source of childcare, as they can have a tendency to be cancelled at short notice, particularly if run by parents. You may need to ensure you have a back-up plan in case this happens, perhaps a friend on stand-by or a place in the after school club.

7.   Childminder/Nanny/Au pair

You may well choose to use a childminder, nanny or au pair to drop off and collect your children from school. This could work particularly well for you if you had someone already caring for your child before they started school, or if you also have younger pre-school children as well.

8.   Holiday play schemes:

Apart from the school holiday clubs, as described above, there are a growing range of holiday play schemes for children to attend at variable costs (often expensive!). They may be in the form of a play scheme run by a large employer for its staff, with a range of activities on offer each day. It could be a sports centre offering sports days that children can book and take part in, or it could be a specialised company running a week of craft, performing arts or sports. A lot of these activities can be great fun and the children won't even realise it is childcare!

Older children

Secondary school children may not need so much care as such, but you probably won't want to leave them all week to their own devices during the holidays. You need to know where they are and that they are in a safe environment. You may want to arrange for them to spend the day with a friend or family member, or book them onto one of the holiday activities mentioned above. Another option could be for them to go away on a residential holiday for young people, if you can afford it.

Finding childcare

This is a classic chicken and egg situation. Do you find the job first or the childcare? Without the job, you can't pay for the childcare but without the childcare, you can't start the job. This is not an easy one. If you are thinking of going back to work, I suggest that you start researching childcare options alongside looking for and applying for jobs. Visit nurseries, childminders or the after-school club at your child's school. Find out what the waiting lists are like.

Here are a few tips:
- Once you get a job offer, book a childcare place straightaway. There may be an immediate vacancy or you may be told how long you will have to wait for a place.
- Book provisional places with more than one childcare provider (as long as you don't have to pay big deposits); if you are happy to take up whichever one comes up first.
- You may need to negotiate a start date with your employer to fit in with the start of your childcare. In any case, it would be reasonable to expect to wait a month before starting work, and if they need to take up references and perhaps organise other checks, it could take them even longer.
- Could you arrange temporary cover to fill the gap, such as your partner taking some time off work, a parent or friend helping out, or contacting a nanny agency for a temporary

nanny? Your partner may be able to take some unpaid parental leave to fill the gap (see below).

- Nurseries will often tell you that they have a three, six or twelve month waiting list, when in reality a place may well come up much sooner than this. Often the time they give is the maximum you are likely to have to wait if everyone on the list above you takes up their place. In reality, many places will not be taken up and you may move up the list quicker than you expect.
- Childcare places will often become available in September as the previous cohort of children move up to school.
- Whilst you are looking for work, see if you can find a place for just one morning or afternoon a week with a childminder or nursery if you can afford it. This will give you valuable time to spend on your job hunting, but you are also likely to be the first person to be offered a place when one comes up. Nurseries and childminders will usually offer newly available places to current families before they offer them to new ones, so get a foot in the door as soon as you can. This approach will also be a gentle introduction for both you and your child into a new childcare environment, assisting the eventual transition to work and more childcare hours.

Settling in to childcare

Starting in a new childcare setting can be an anxious time for both you and your child. These tips may help the settling in process:

- Visit the new childcare setting with your child before you leave them there on their own, to help them to get to know the new place and their new carers. Use this chance to help the childcare get to know your child and their routine and for you to find out more about what happens during the day.
- Say goodbye to your child and reassure them that you will come back. If they are old enough to understand, tell them when you will be back.
- If your child cries when you leave, don't be tempted to come back to check up on them. Trust the childcare to look after them. Most children will have stopped crying a few minutes after you have left and got distracted by all the new toys and children. If you are worried, ring an hour later to check on them.
- On your first day in your new job you may prefer your partner or a close family member to care for your child, so

that your first day back at work is not overshadowed by your child's first full day in a new childcare setting.

- Try to hide your anxiety and insecurity when you drop your child off, as they are likely to pick up on your stress at leaving them.

What to do when it all goes wrong

So you've got your perfectly sorted childcare arrangements and your child is settled, but what do you do when it all goes wrong? Disasters can come in a number of forms: perhaps your childminder or nanny is sick, or your child is sick and can't go to the childminder or nursery. Maybe there is a teacher training day at school (at least you should have warning of this), or the school or nursery is closed for the day because of snow. Sometimes it is a little harder to predict. I remember once being thrown by my children's school being closed due to a sewage flood and only finding out about it when a friend rang me at 8.20 in the morning. At least with snow days you have an idea that the school might close! Or maybe you suddenly have a work commitment that doesn't fit in with your childcare, such as a training course that finishes at 6pm an hour away from home, or an important meeting or conference you need to go to that falls on a day when you don't normally work. Or perhaps your childminder suddenly decides to stop childminding (as happened to me), or your nanny gets another job. How can you deal with these situations?

- Ultimately your primary commitment lies with your child, not your employer. If there's no childcare for your child, you can't go to work.
- Can your partner take the day off? Don't forget, it's his child too, so don't let the whole responsibility for childcare fall to you.
- Call in some favours. Now's the time to ask your friends or family members to help you out. If you've done the same for them at another time it will be easier to ask. Perhaps pre-empt the situation by having an arrangement with another friend who works part-time whereby you agree to help each other out in emergencies or perhaps have a friend who doesn't work to be available to help when you need it, maybe in return for evening babysitting.
- Be honest with your employer. If your employer is fairly family friendly, they may well be understanding of your situation. You could offer to make the hours up at another

time, perhaps reorganising any appointments you may have had, or take it out of your annual leave. With any luck, they may just be generous and tell you not to worry about it.

- You do have the legal right to take unpaid time off work to deal with an unexpected event to do with your dependants (ie children). This could include your child being sick, or your childcare arrangements falling through. This would normally be expected to be for no more than a day or two at a time.
- You may be tempted to call in sick for fear of your employer not being impressed by being let down. Think carefully before you take this option, as it may backfire!
- If you know you really need to be in work the day your child falls sick, and you can find no one to help, try calling a nanny agency to arrange for a temporary nanny. This can often be done at surprisingly short notice.

Parental leave

Any working parent is allowed to take up to thirteen weeks of unpaid parental leave for each child until their fifth birthday. This would normally be taken in one lump, at a time to be mutually agreed with your employer. Remember that this is available, as it may tide you over some tricky times, such as your nanny handing in their notice, your child going into hospital for an operation, or for your partner to take when you start work, if you have a gap before your childcare starts.

Points to ponder

- Look at as many childcare options as you can.
- Put your child's name down with a childcare provider as soon as you can.
- Choose childcare that you know is right for you and your family, don't be swayed by everyone else's opinion or the current trends.
- Ask around for recommendations.
- Forget the guilt complex, just enjoy the time you have with your child.
- Let your child settle in gradually if possible, starting with just an hour at a time.
- Make sure you get any help with childcare costs that you are entitled to (see next chapter).
- Ask lots of questions when you visit child carers, ask about their views on discipline, feeding, entertaining your

children or anything else that matters to you.

- Trust your 'gut instinct' as to whether a child carer or childcare setting feels right for your child.

Information

Nannies	www.nannyjob.co.uk
Childminders	www.familyinformationservices.org.uk
Au pairs	www.iapa.org
Information on childcare providers in any part of the country	childcarefinder.direct.gov.uk or ring the National Childcare Helpline on 0800 2346 346

Chapter Twelve

Benefits and finances

You will have a number of reasons for going back to work, but one of them will no doubt be financial. You may well be fed up with relying on benefits, your partner's income, or maintenance payments from your ex and want or need to make your own money. When considering jobs to apply for, it's important that you know how much you will take home at the end of the month, whether you are entitled to any other help from the government and what costs you are going to have to pay out on childcare and other expenses. At the end of the day will your family be any better off financially? If not, you may choose not to go back to work for now.

However, finances are not the only reason for going back to work, and I know many women who have gone back to work even though they know they are actually no better off at the end of the month. There are many reasons for this, which we touched on in Chapter Two. It is worth bearing in mind that by working now, you may be better off in the future. Firstly, if you pay part of your salary into a pension scheme, you will hopefully reap the benefits of that in years to come, albeit possibly in decades' time! Secondly, by working now you may be investing in your career, perhaps doing a low level job and gaining experience that will lead to promotion and better pay in a year or two's time. Another argument could be that if your dream job comes up and you are lucky enough to get it, then take your chance, even if it is costing you now. By the time the children have started school, that opportunity may not be available, so it may be worth taking it now, whilst you can.

How much will I take home?

You've seen a job advertised and the salary is given, but you have no idea how much money you will have left at the end of the month. You will need to consider the following issues:

Part-time salaries: the advertised salary will normally be that given for a full-time job. If, for example, a salary is advertised as '£20,000 (pro-rata)', this is the amount you would get if you worked full time. If you are working part-time, you will get a proportion of this dependent on the number of hours worked. So if you were working four days a week, you would get 80% of £20,000, which is £16,000. If you know you will be working 16 hours a week, you would need to know what the company considered to be a full-time week before you can work out what you would actually get. Full-time is usually considered to be anywhere between 35 and 40 hours a week, but 37 and ½ hours would be a good guess.

Tax and National Insurance: once you've worked out how much you will get a year, you need to work out how much tax and national insurance you will be paying. Tax and National Insurance rates and thresholds change with every annual government budget, so rather than go into detail here, the easiest thing to do is to use an online calculator such as www.thesalarycalculator.co.uk This will quickly work out for you what you will take home per month or year after tax and national insurance at the current rates.

Other benefits and tax credits: bear in mind that these also change on a regular basis and at the time of writing, with a new government, these details may not be accurate for long. Check the websites given for up-to-date facts.
Child Benefit: if your children are living at home, then you will probably already be getting child benefit, and this will not change by you going back to work. You should receive a fixed amount, not dependent on your income.
Child Tax Credit: this is a means tested payment for families with children. 90% of families are entitled to some child tax credit. If you are already receiving it the amount you receive may change if you start working, so make sure you let the tax office know of your changed circumstances.
Working Tax Credit: is also means tested and usually only paid to families on low incomes. It is designed to top up the income of families where one or both partners are working 16 or more hours a week. It was brought in to reduce the 'benefit trap' where families found themselves worse off in work than on benefits. In some cases you may also be eligible for help with up to 80% of your childcare costs. In theory it should ensure that you are better off in work. You would generally only be entitled to Working Tax Credit if your income is fairly low. For more (up-to-date) information on the above benefits and tax credits and to check your entitlement, use the websites listed at the end of the chapter.

Pensions:
You may choose to start (or re-start) paying into a pension scheme. This will be another slice taken out of your take home pay, but hopefully you'll see it again one day! You may be paying into a

private pension scheme, or if the company you are applying to work for has its own pension scheme, the human resources department will usually be happy to give you details.

Other changes to finances
You may need to consider other factors when calculating the net benefits of returning to work. As well as extra childcare costs, you may also need to start paying for:
- Smart work clothes.
- Transport or possibly a second car.
- Lunchtime sandwiches, or will you make your own?
- Occasional ready meals in the evenings, if you don't have time to cook meals from scratch.
- Expensive nights out with work colleagues, rather than a night in with a DVD and a bottle of wine with your 'mum friends'.
- School dinners for your children, to save time on making sandwiches in the mornings.

Financial help with childcare

Many women are put off working when the children are young because the costs of childcare seem just too much in relation to their take home pay. Changes in government legislation have altered the situation in recent years, and for some people it has improved. For others, however, it is still prohibitive. Check the facts first before you assume it is too expensive. Possible sources of help with childcare expenses may include:
- Free nursery entitlement: every three and four year old is entitled to 15 hours of free early learning a week for 38 weeks per year. These hours are available in OfSted registered nurseries and pre-schools as well as some private nursery schools and registered childminders.
- There are some free places for two year olds who meet certain criteria. Contact your local Families Information Service to find out more.
- As mentioned above, depending on your income, you may be able to get help with up to 80% of your childcare costs through working tax credit. Go to Inland Revenue website for a claim form or to use their online tax credits calculator.
- Childcare vouchers are offered by some employers where you pay for registered childcare out of your salary, saving you part of your tax and National Insurance costs. You will

need to talk to your employer when you have one, to find out if they are part of this scheme, or encourage them to get involved. Childcare vouchers must be used in 'registered or approved' childcare, which does not usually include nannies or care by family members.

Where to get help

If you are concerned about your income or are in debt, then make sure you get some help. Your local Citizen's Advice Bureau will be able to help you. Or ring the National Debtline on 0808 808 4000. Don't let it get worse. Ask for help.

Points to ponder

- Make sure you know (roughly) what your take home pay will be before you accept a job offer.
- Ensure you claim any benefits, tax credits or other financial help that you are entitled to.
- Get help and advice with any financial matters should you need it.

Information

To calculate take home pay	www.thesalarycalculator.co.uk
Online benefits and tax credits calculator	www.turn2us.org.uk
Inland revenue website to make claims for benefits and tax credits	www.hmrc.gov.uk
For further information on benefits, tax credits, tax and national insurance	www.direct.gov.uk (benefits section)
A comprehensive and helpful selection of fact sheets on finances for families. They also have a simple to use Tax Credit Estimator.	www.workingfamilies.org.uk
Local Families Information Services	www.familyinformationservices.org.uk
Citizen's Advice Bureau	www.citizensadvice.org.uk
National Debtline	0808 808 4000

Chapter Thirteen

Positive communication: How to be assertive

Why is assertiveness important to women returners?

When you are lucky enough to have found a job that suits you, starting work will lead to big changes in your life and the life of your family. This next section is aimed at helping you with some of the changes that will come as a result of starting work. I believe assertiveness is a hugely useful tool to help you survive and thrive in everyday life. Assertiveness is all about communicating clearly, making it known what you need and think, whilst listening to and respecting what other people need.

When you start a new job, you may need to be assertive with your boss when a meeting which was due to finish at 5pm runs over; you need to be out the door in five minutes to get to nursery in time and your boss wants you to stay till the end of the meeting. If you've taken on the bulk of the household tasks whilst you've been at home and your family is starting to take you for granted, things are going to have to change when you go back to work. You will need to be assertive with your family – asking your children to tidy their bedroom or lay the table and your partner to take more responsibility for cooking and cleaning.

Types of behaviour

When looking at communication, there are generally considered to be four types of behaviour: aggressive, assertive, passive and passive–aggressive.

Aggressive behaviour
- Expressing feelings and opinions in a way that puts other people down.
- Not considering the rights, needs and feelings of others.
- Trying to get your own way, whatever it takes.

- Using an angry tone of voice and threatening body language and possibly violence.
- Not admitting when you are wrong.
- 'I'm OK, you're not OK'.

Assertive behaviour
- Being open and honest.
- Listening to and respecting other people's point of view.
- Expressing views clearly, whilst not assuming you are right.
- Being able to resolve conflict, and negotiating a workable solution.
- Standing up for one's self and not being trampled on and ignored.
- Being able to ask for what you need in a respectful way.
- Respect for self and others.
- Admitting when you are wrong.
- Being able to say no.
- 'I'm OK, you're OK'.

Passive behaviour
- Agreeing with other people all the time and not expressing your own views.
- Avoiding conflict or argument.
- Not being able to say 'no' when you want to.
- Not standing up for yourself and asking for what you need.
- Putting other's needs first at the expense of your own.
- Finding it hard to make decisions.
- Needing other's approval.
- Apologising too much.
- 'You're OK, I'm not OK'.

Passive-aggressive (or manipulative) behaviour
- Neither respecting the views or needs of others or yourself.
- Not asking directly for what you want.
- Trying to get what you want by playing games, making hints and making others feel guilty.
- Often used by people who feel insecure and are lacking in confidence.
- 'You're not OK, I'm not OK'.

The following diagram may help to explain these different types of behaviour:

The Mum's Guide to Returning to Work

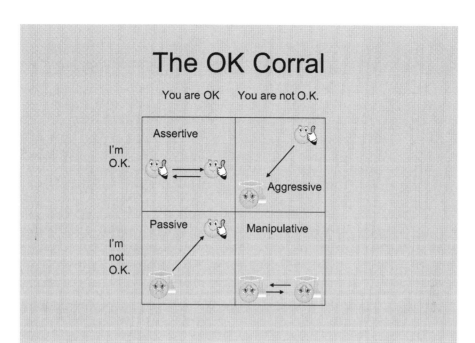

Adapted from 'I'm OK – You're OK' by Thomas Harris [1]

How assertive are you?

I hope you are getting a feel for the four types of behaviour; perhaps you can picture yourself or others in the above descriptions. Let's look at some common situations and think about how you might tend to behave in each of them.

How assertive are you?

1. Your partner wants to go camping in France for your main summer holiday, whilst you'd rather go to an all inclusive hotel in Spain, where you know you'd get a proper break. Do you:

a. Agree to go camping, but spend the whole holiday moaning about it?

b. Go along with his ideas, just to keep the peace?

c. Say how you feel and what you would like – try to come up with a compromise?

d. Flatly refuse to go?

---

2.   A friend asks to borrow a brand new book from you, but you know they never give anything back:

a.   Tell them that you've already agreed to lend it to someone else, even if this isn't true?

b.   Go ahead and lend it anyway?

c.   Tell them that you are not keen to lend books out as sometimes you don't get them back. Suggest that they might find a cheap copy second hand on Amazon.

d.   Say there is no way you are going to lend them a book as you didn't get back the last three books you lent them.?

3.   A friend has been rather cool with you lately and you wonder if you have offended them somehow. Do you:

a.   Bitch about them to everyone you know?

b.   Do nothing; they don't have to be your friend?

c.   Invite them round for a coffee and politely ask if they are OK, as they seem to have been a bit cool towards you recently.

d.   Have it out with them to provoke an argument?

4.   In a shop, you are kept waiting to be served while shop assistants are gossiping. Do you:

a.   Mutter under your breath something about poor service?

b.   Wait patiently to be noticed?

c.   Approach the assistants and ask pleasantly for help?

d.   Start shouting and swearing about how hard it is to get good service these days?

How did you respond?
Mostly a   Passive-aggressive behaviour
Mostly b   Passive behaviour
Mostly c   Assertive behaviour
Mostly d   Aggressive behaviour

What kind of behaviour do you tend to adopt? The chances are that you behave differently in different situations, depending on who you are with and how confident you feel. I know that I tend to adopt an aggressive approach with my children when they leave their coats and shoes on the floor when coming in from school for the fifth time in a week. I adopt a passive approach with a friend of mine who is a little intimidating and forthright in her opinions, meaning that I just go along with what she thinks, rather than standing up for my own views.

The benefits of being assertive

You may be like me and behave differently in different situations, but I know that my intention is always to behave in an assertive way, because I have found it to be so much more effective and pleasant for everyone. If I am assertive with my children about tidying, I will praise them when they do (albeit rarely) put their shoes away, explain to them calmly and clearly what I expect of them and why, and tell them the benefits to themselves of doing what they are told ie a happy, calm mum, who won't interrupt them in the middle of a game telling them to put their shoes away. The result will be happy, confident children who are not scared of their mum, but are learning to be independent adults, I in turn will not feel guilty and frustrated for shouting at them and we'll all have a tidy house (hopefully)!

By expressing my views to my friend, I will feel more positive about myself, may have an interesting debate looking at both sides of an issue and she will probably end up having more respect for me, for having stood up for myself. If she chooses not to speak to me anymore because she doesn't like my views, then maybe that's no loss!

Being assertive will help you to get what you want and need, enable you to get your point across, be a useful tool in resolving difficult situations and lead to a greater degree of respect from other people. But it's your choice. You don't have to be assertive and there may be occasions where you actively choose not to be.

How to communicate assertively

1.   Listen:
Try to understand the situation from the other person's point of view. Use active listening skills (open questions, being non-judgemental) to try to find out more. The issue may be more complex than is first suggested.

2.   Demonstrate understanding
Reflect back what you think the other person is saying. Eg 'So you are not happy about …..'. This gives the other person a chance to agree that you've got it right or correct it if you have it wrong.

3.   Explanation

Explain the situation as you see it. Be as objective as possible. Keep to the point – don't be tempted to bring in other issues. Be brief.

4.   Feelings

Acknowledge your own feelings and own them as your responsibility. Don't accuse the other person of making you feel anything. For example, say *'I'm angry'* not *'you make me angry'*. Empathise with the other person's feelings or situation; try to look at it from their point of view: *'I realise that you really need someone to help with this'*.

5.   Needs

Outline clearly what it is that you want to happen. Dropping hints doesn't always work! Being clear about what you want to happen increases the possibility of getting it and minimises the chance of being misunderstood.

6.   Consequences

This could be a positive consequence *'If we can sort out this situation it will be a lot easier for all of us'* or *'I would be very grateful if ….'*. If this doesn't work, you could use a negative consequence: *'If you persist with …. I will no longer be able to ……'*

7.   Joint solutions

Where there is a gap between what you want and what others want, you need to negotiate a joint solution or a compromise. If you want plan A and they want plan B, could there be a plan C that you are both happy with?

Remember you are aiming for a win-win situation; 'I am O.K. - you are O.K.'
Adapted from Springboard Women's Development Workbook[2]

When you know you need to be assertive, try following the approach above. It may not feel natural to start with but like learning any language, fluency comes with time and practice. You might want to write down or think through in your head what you need to say to someone before you do it. An assertive conversation using some of the points above might look something like this:

Explanation:	*'I bought this jumper from you last week and after wearing it just twice it has bobbles all over it, so I am no longer able to wear it for work.'*
Feelings:	*'I am very disappointed, because it cost a lot and I have come to expect better quality from this shop. I know we are in a recession and I realise that you need to make ends meet …..'*
Needs:	*'…. but I really would appreciate it if you could give me a refund.'*
Consequences:	*'I would be delighted to use your store again if we can come to an agreement.'*
Joint solutions:	this is the conversation that would follow where you come to a mutual agreement and hopefully get the refund.

Assertiveness doesn't always work, particularly when we are up against aggressive people who are out to get their own way regardless. However, I believe that you are far more likely to solve a problem by using an assertive approach and if you still don't solve it, at least you will have preserved your self respect by trying.

Assertiveness rights

What might encourage you to be assertive is choosing to believe that you have the 'right' to be assertive. You may also choose to believe that you have the right to say no, the right to express your opinions, the right to ask for what you need and the right to make mistakes. If you choose to take on board these rights (or indeed any others), you might also like to think about the equal and opposite responsibilities that go with them. You may therefore feel that you have a responsibility to allow other people to be assertive, to say 'no', to express their opinions, to ask for what they need and to make mistakes.

How to say 'no'

Being able to say 'no' is one aspect of assertive communication that I think is more useful and powerful then any other I can think of. How many times has someone rung you up and asked you to babysit, to help on a committee or to go out for the evening with them and you've automatically said 'yes' without thinking about it? In cases like this you may well have instantly regretted it the moment you put down the phone.

I think the key to saying 'no' is being able to choose when your answer should be 'yes' and when it should be 'no'. Notice your gut reaction to a question and think carefully before you respond. If you're not sure, ask for some time to think about it and promise to get back with a response shortly. This will help you to make your choice as well as thinking how to word your response carefully if it is indeed 'no'. I remember the first time I ran an assertiveness workshop with a group of women; we concentrated on looking at how to say 'no'. I don't think I really emphasised that we don't have to say 'no' in every situation, but need to work out when it is most appropriate to say 'no'. At the end of the session these women went off all excited, having collectively agreed that they were all going to say 'no' to their husbands when they asked them to cook their supper. I'm glad that they left feeling empowered, but hope that it didn't lead to too many divorces!

If your answer is 'no', say so honestly. Give your response without excessive excuses and apologies. Acknowledge the other person's needs and remember that you both have rights. Offer a compromise or an alternative solution if you can. Don't beat around the bush with your answer or make up an excuse, as apart from possibly being unbelievable, it may only get you into trouble later. If the other person won't take no for an answer and keeps nagging you, use what is called the 'broken record technique' and repeat your answer as many times as needed, without getting dragged into a long drawn-out discussion.

Essentially you are following the assertive communication guidelines laid out above. A conversation might look something like this:

> Sarah: 'Hi Bekki, I was wondering if you are able to babysit on Friday night please?'
>
> Bekki: 'No, I'm sorry Sarah, I can't babysit on Friday, I've promised to spend the evening with my husband. I realise you need to find someone urgently, but how about trying Helen's daughter, I know she's always keen to earn some money. You know I'll happily do it another time if you need me.'
>
> Sarah: 'Oh go on Bekki, you know you owe me a favour, I really don't want to pay someone.'
>
> Bekki: 'No, I can't do it on Friday, I've promised my husband'.
>
> Sarah: 'Can't you change your plans and see him another evening?'
>
> Bekki: 'No, I can't babysit on Friday, I've promised my husband'.
>
> Sarah: 'Oh fair enough!'

Go out and practice it

The best way to be assertive is to go out and practice it. Think about situations you want to change, work out what you want to achieve and how you might go about asking for it and give it a go. It might feel tricky at first, but keep trying.

This chapter has really only been an introduction to the basics of assertiveness. If you are interested in it there are lots of very good books on the subject (see below). Or you might think about finding a local course on assertiveness I'm sure you won't regret it.

Points to ponder

- Try to recognise the types of behaviour you use in different situations.
- What factors might hold you back from being more assertive?
- Try being assertive in small situations first, before trying more challenging ones.
- Plan out a 'script' of what you might want to say to someone before approaching them about an issue.
- You have the 'right' to be assertive. You also have the 'right' to not be assertive.

Reading

Windy Dryden and Daniel Constantinou, *Assertiveness Step by Step,* Sheldon, 2004

Gael Lindenfield, *Assert Yourself: Simple Steps to Getting What You Want*, Element, 2001

Liz Willis & Jenny Daisley, *Springboard Women's Development Workbook,* Hawthorn Press, 2008

Chapter Fourteen

Time management: how to fit 36 hours into a 24 hour day

Going from being a full-time mum with children at home or at school, to becoming a working mum, whether full or part-time, will inevitably lead to some changes. I shall make the assumption that whilst at home you have had primary responsibility in your family for at least some of the cooking, cleaning, washing, gardening, finances, shopping, homework help and DIY in your household. When you start working, these activities will still have to happen, but there may need to be a change in how you get them done. Effective time management will enable you to find ways of getting these tasks done, whilst still having time to spend with your children and go to work. At the moment, you may feel that your hours are full and you couldn't fit anything more into your day, so starting a job may seem impossible.

You might find it helpful to do a 'time audit' to help you analyse how you spend your time in a typical week. Make a chart and include whatever categories are relevant to you. These could include: housework, sleeping, time for yourself, time with partner, time with children, watching TV, voluntary work, exercise, time with friends, evening class, taking children to school or other activities. Make a note of how long you spend on each activity every day, and add it up over a week. Look at the results, do they surprise you? Apart from sleeping, what do you spend the most time on? What things could you spend less time on in the future? Do you spend any time on yourself?

In order to start paid work, you will need to find some extra hours somewhere. Where are they going to come from? I'm sure we've all had days when we wish we had more than 24 hours, but with effective time management you will be able to fit in far more than you thought possible. Time management boils down to three things: being more efficient with the things you do, cutting out things you don't need to do and (counter-intuitively) spending more time on yourself. Let's look at each in turn.

How to be more efficient in what you do

If you've got pre-school children and are at home all the time with them, then you've probably become pretty good at spending your time efficiently and will be a dab hand at multi-tasking: taking the children to the supermarket with you, making cleaning into a game and finding ways to occupy the children whilst you cook the tea. If, however, your children are now at school and you are home all day, you may have forgotten some of these skills and find yourself letting the jobs expand to fill the time available. If this is your problem, look at some of these tips for using your time more efficiently:

- Make lists of things to do, to buy, people to call. Then prioritise what really matters on the list and tick it off as you work through it. Are there some things on the list that don't really need to be done?
- Multi-task – cycle somewhere instead of driving, so that you are exercising as well as getting somewhere you need to be (possibly saving money, time and the environment in the process).
- Discover your best time of day. Are you lark or an owl? Do you have most patience, energy and enthusiasm in the morning or evening? Save the most demanding tasks for when you are at your peak.
- Fill the gaps. Are there times when you can get a little job done whilst waiting for the kettle to boil or sitting in the doctor's waiting room? You may prefer to leave those gaps empty to give you some head space.
- Combine tasks when going out. Can you post that letter on the way to collect the children from school, instead of doing a special trip?
- Lower your standards – does the house really need to be as clean and tidy as you are used to it being?

> When I went back to work it was hard to get everything done in the much reduced time at home, but actually I still had lots of time compared to people working full-time. I found that I was more efficient with the home tasks because I just had to be.
>
> Celia

Spend less time on certain things

Are there some things you are doing now that don't need to be done, or could someone else do them? Think through the following ideas:
- Online shopping for groceries, clothes, books etc.
- Pay someone to help with housework - cleaning, ironing, gardening.
- Learn to say 'no' to those requests which you don't want to do or don't have time for (be assertive, read Chapter Thirteen if you haven't done already).
- Cook in bulk and freeze the leftovers. Simplify the meals you cook.
- Delegate - to your partner, your children, family and friends as appropriate. Don't let your family take you for granted, but ask them to do their share of work around the home. Try not to feel guilty about asking your children to help, as they will learn life skills and independence in the process, as well as having a less stressed mum!
- What can you cut out of your day? Will your life really be any worse if you stop watching that soap opera you are addicted to? That's not to say watching TV doesn't have a role in helping you to relax though!

'Life's too short to stuff a mushroom.'

Shirley Conran

Spend more time on yourself

This may feel like a luxury and something you don't have time for. However, in order to function effectively in the rest of your life, you need to set aside time for yourself, in order to recharge your batteries. You will benefit from it as much as those around you. Encourage your family to respect your need for time to yourself. Have a think about activities you could take up that will give you time for yourself, for example:
- Sport – watching
- Sport – playing
- Eating out
- Keeping fit
- Cooking
- Cinema

- Hobby or craft
- Gardening
- Shopping
- Reading
- DIY
- Studying
- Music – playing or listening
- Evening class
- Going for a walk
- Meeting up with friends
- Having a long bath
- Ringing a friend
- Watching a DVD
- Going away for an occasional weekend on your own or with your partner
- Voluntary or community activity.

When my children were younger, I got so fed up with spending time looking after other people's needs that I decided to join a choir. I've joined a gospel choir and have a fantastic time singing and meeting new people. I've rigidly stuck to my choir night for the past six years now, and even get a babysitter if my husband is out. I find singing a really positive, uplifting experience, but also enjoy just being 'Bekki', rather than someone's mum. I also think I'm setting a good role model to my children, helping them to see that I believe I am important too and that my life doesn't entirely revolve round them. I'm also convinced that spending time on myself helps me feel more positive in myself and more effective in how I spend the rest of my time. I see it as an investment.

What could you do to ensure that you invest time in yourself every week?

The Mayonnaise Jar

When things in your life seem almost too much to handle, when 24 hours in a day are not enough, remember the mayonnaise jar... and its story...

A lecturer stood before her philosophy class and had some items in front of her. When the class began, wordlessly, she picked up a very large and empty mayonnaise jar and proceeded to fill it with golf balls. She then asked the students if the jar was full. They agreed that it was. The lecturer then picked up a box of pebbles and poured them into the jar. She shook the jar lightly. The pebbles rolled into the open areas between the golf balls. She then asked the students again if the jar was full. They agreed it was.

The lecturer next picked up a box of sand and poured it into the jar. Of course, the sand filled up everything else. She asked once more if the jar was full. The students responded with an emphatic 'yes.' The lecturer then produced two cups of coffee from under the table and poured the entire contents into the jar, effectively filling the empty space between the sand. The students laughed. 'Now,' said the lecturer, as the laughter subsided, 'I want you to recognise that this jar represents your life.

The golf balls are the important things. Your family, your children, your faith, your health, your friends, and your favourite passions. Things that if everything else was lost and only they remained, your life would still be full. The pebbles are the other things that matter. Your job, your house, and your car.

The sand is everything else. The small stuff. 'If you put the sand into the jar first,' she continued, 'there is no room for the pebbles or the golf balls. The same goes for life. If you spend all your time and energy on the small stuff, you will never have room for the things that are important to you.

Pay attention to the things that are critical to your happiness. Play with your children. Take time to stay healthy. Take your partner out to dinner. Go for a walk in the sunshine. There will always be time to clean the house and do the ironing. Take care of the golf balls first, the things that really matter. Set your priorities. The rest is just sand.'

One of the students raised her hand and inquired what the coffee represented. The lecturer smiled. 'I'm glad you asked. It just goes to show you that no matter how full your life may seem, there's always room for a couple of cups of coffee with a friend.'
Anon

Dealing with stress

Any major change in your life can lead to stress, so returning to work will certainly be a big change for you. Or even when you just have too much to do and it feels like everything is falling apart, you can suffer from stress. Signs of stress can include not sleeping, getting run down and sick, being irritable, feeling low, crying, losing your temper, overeating or drinking too much. Stress can be caused by a huge range of things, but generally it's by things over which we have no control. If the symptoms of stress you are experiencing become too much, make sure you ask for help from appropriate professionals such as your GP. The following tips might be helpful though:

- **Think it through:** before you go into a situation that may be stressful, take time to think the situation through, step by step. Try to work out exactly what it is that is likely to make you feel under stress. Is there anything you can do to make the situation less stressful? Sometimes just thinking through a situation like this can help to reduce the pressure associated with it.
- **Plan your time**: if you feel under stress because your days seem hectic and overcrowded, or because time seems to drag by without purpose, try drawing up a timetable for your day. Decide what it is you want to do – and what you can leave for another time – and when you are going to do it. Look at tips from the time management exercise.
- **Talk things over**: find someone you can trust – it may be a friend or family member, or it could be a trained adviser or counsellor – and make time to talk things over with him or her. This can help to relieve the pressure on you. Let yourself cry if you need to, as this can help to release pent up emotions.
- **Exercise:** making time for any kind of exercise will make you feel calmer. Yoga and tai chi can be particularly good for lowering stress. Exercise burns up adrenaline and produces helpful chemicals and positive feelings in the brain.
- **Think positively:** try to be detached from the situation, step back and look from the outside at issues causing stress. You may not be able to change the stressful situation, but you can change your reaction to it. Is there a positive aspect to the situation that you can focus on? Remove yourself from the situation that causes stress, leave the building and go for a short walk to get some fresh air and exercise.
- **Humour:** 'Laughter is the best medicine': laughter releases chemicals in the brain which make us feel better and can distract us from our worries. Try watching a comedy programme on the TV.
- **Sleep:** get more sleep - the world looks different when you are not completely exhausted. Powernap if you can - many people swear by the rejuvenating effects of a short 20 minute sleep in the middle of the day.
- **Diet:** A healthy balanced diet will reduce your susceptibility to stress.
- **Take time out to relax:** if you feel you're too busy to relax, then you're probably too busy! On the other hand, even if we've

The Mum's Guide to Returning to Work

got time on our hands, we can often find it hard to give ourselves 'permission' to relax. Make sure you build in time to do something that relaxes you, whether it's soaking in a hot bath, reading a good book or magazine, or doing a relaxation exercise.

Points to ponder

- How can you create the extra hours you need to fit a job into what might already seem a hectic life?
- Don't be scared to delegate to the rest of the family.
- Try saying 'no' every now and then.
- Don't forget to spend time on yourself.
- Recognise that the world will not fall apart if your clothes aren't ironed and there are a few specks of dirt on the floor.
- Be aware of the first signs of stress and take action to deal with it.

Reading

Julia Hobsbawm, *The See-Saw: 100 Ideas For Work-Life Balance: 100 Recipes For Work-Life Balance,* Atlantic books, 2009

Chapter Fifteen

Women from Overseas

Cambridge is a far more cosmopolitan city than you might expect. My daughter is one of the few children in her class who are not bi-lingual, having friends from Japan, Mexico, Brazil, Slovakia, Germany, France, Russia and Korea as well as the USA. Whether it is families coming to work or study at the university or to work at one of the many hi-tech companies in the city, Cambridge is full of people from overseas and, in my opinion, a more interesting and vibrant city as a result. Cambridge is not unusual: in 2008 over ½ million people arrived in the UK to work or study. [1]

Many women come to the city to accompany their partner who is working or studying and often they end up at CWRC where they come to learn English or to study another course. My role involves supporting them to find work and this is often a tricky challenge for them. On top of the usual barriers we have looked at before, other issues may include the legality of working in the UK, recognition of overseas qualifications, lack of English, experience of work being different in another country and referees being based abroad. We will have a look at each of these issues in turn.

The whole process of finding work can be very different in other countries than it is in the UK. I've spoken to women from countries where a certificate of employment or an appraisal report would be used instead of a reference and others where interviews don't exist at all and the best candidate on paper is given the job. In another case those candidates who are not offered the job are given a period of time when they can object to the job being offered to the preferred candidate before a contract is finally signed. The whole job hunting process in the UK may well be different from your own country, so if you are from overseas you will need to understand how the whole process works here. I hope previous chapters will have helped somewhat with this. Let's look at some of the other issues you may be facing.

Are you legally allowed to work here?

I won't go into too much detail on this issue, as it is a complicated, specialist area and I don't want to give wrong advice. In any case, the law can change quickly. In most, but not quite all, cases, if you are from the European Economic Area (EEA) and Switzerland you are permitted to come to, live in and work in the UK. If you are not from the EEA, it should say in your passport whether or not you have permission to work here.

Suffice it to say, you will probably know if you are legally permitted to work in the UK, so you should not try to work here if you are not allowed to. If you are not sure and you need more information, then look at the government's Border Agency website for more detailed information.

Is your English good enough?

Unless you come from an English speaking country, the chances are that English is not your first language and you may or may not be fluent in it. Employers are generally not there to help you; they are there to fill a vacancy with the best possible candidate. If two equally well qualified, skilled and experienced candidates attend a job interview, but one is fluent in English and the other is not, the chances are that the fluent candidate will get the job.

This choice might sometimes be interpreted as racism or prejudice, and indeed sometimes that might be the case. However, if you use some words or phrases inappropriately and your accent is so strong that people have to really concentrate to understand you, an employer will not be sure that you will be able to communicate clearly with clients, customers and colleagues. Depending on the job, an employer may also need to be sure that any written communication is free from grammatical and spelling mistakes and that there is sufficient knowledge of any technical language needed.

If you have a reasonable level of English, you may want to take a test to show employers the level you have achieved. The IELTS (International English Language Testing System) is a well recognised test which gives you a level for listening, reading, writing and speaking. You get a banding of 1 to 9 for each area, with level 6 being considered competent. The test usually costs around £100 to take and can be taken at any one of over 44 test centres throughout the UK. Go to the IELTS website to find out more about the test and where you can take it.

You may feel that you need to improve your English before you start to look for work. Indeed, I believe the main reason that people who have English as a second or other language find it hard to find work in the UK is because their English is just not good enough. Do not despair though, as it will improve. If you have the time, concentrate on this before you start to look for work, otherwise you may have to settle for a job at a lower level than you are used to.

Most local further education colleges will run ESOL (English for Speakers of Other Languages) courses. These will tend to cover English for everyday life and are subsidised by the government, making them fairly affordable. Use the 'Find a Course' section of the Next Step website to find a suitable course. Course providers will be able to do an assessment with you to find out your level of English, waiting lists for ESOL courses can sometimes be long. If you cannot find or are not eligible for a local ESOL course, you could look at English courses at private language schools, although this is likely to be more expensive. The English in Britain website can give you information on where to find a private language school.

If you can't find a course near you, if you don't have childcare in place to do a course, or it's just too expensive, look for other ways to improve your English. Take up any opportunity you can to speak English with other people. Perhaps you could try talking to other mums at toddler groups or at the school gate, join an exercise class or get involved in an activity where you can get to speak to people. Unfortunately this is not always easy and people you speak to may not always be as friendly as you might hope.

An excellent suggestion given to me by an ESOL tutor I know is to listen to the radio, in particular Radio 4. If you don't know it, programmes on BBC Radio 4 consist mostly of talking, rather than music. They may have discussions on politics, current affairs, or perhaps a play or arts programme. Listen to the radio as you go about your daily activities and absorb the words, phrases used and the accent. If you are brave (and no one else is listening) try copying what the presenters are saying, copying their accent as accurately as you can. Even if you feel silly doing this, it will really help.

All your work experience is overseas

I often speak to women who are not sure whether to include jobs they have done overseas on application forms and CVs. The answer is yes! Employers want to know what you have done before, what skills you have developed and what experience you have. This is still valid, even if you have done it abroad. Perhaps you have ten years' experience of retail management in another country. Yes, shops will operate differently in other countries and there may be legal issues such as VAT (sales tax) which differ, but customers are the same the world over and your experience of managing staff, customer service, displaying stock and using a till is still valid experience.

Make sure you explain your previous jobs in a clear way on CVs and application forms. Job roles can be very different in other countries and you need to make sure employers understand what you did. Ask an English friend if the way you have described it makes sense to them. Make sure job titles are in English, and even if you cannot find an exact translation, try to translate it as accurately as possible.

Having said that, it is also good if you can show that you have some experience of working in the UK. This will show that you have an understanding of how things work in your particular field in this country and it will also give you the chance to get a recent reference from someone who is UK-based. To do this you might like to consider trying to find some unpaid work experience. Contact employers with your CV and offer to work for a short period of time for no pay. If they are able to offer you something, you will get some valuable work experience to put on your CV, as well as a reference.

Overseas qualifications are not understood or recognised

If your qualifications are from the European Union, then they should be recognised in the UK. So for example, if you are a qualified doctor, nurse, teacher or physiotherapist, your qualification should be considered equal to a British qualification and you should be able to practice in that field here.

If your qualification is from outside the EU you may need to get an official conversion of it, so that employers will understand how your qualification relates to a British one. NARIC (The National Academic Recognition Information Centre) will be able to provide you with a 'Letter of Comparability' to enable employers to understand your qualification. It both translates the qualification into English and explains how it relates and compares to an equivalent British qualification. At the time of writing this costs just under £50.

In some professions, you may be able to do further studying to 'top up' your qualification if needed. Again, have a look at the Advice Resources website under 'Job Profiles' to find out about professional bodies in your field where you can find out more about whether your qualification would be accepted and where you could go to top it up if needed.

Play to your strengths

So far in this chapter we have looked at all the things that may be holding you back from finding work in the UK, but perhaps there are things you can offer that are strengths.

- If you speak another language fluently, maybe this could be useful. Could you offer one-to-one tuition in your language on a private basis or look at finding opportunities to teach it in local colleges?

- Translation and interpretation is often needed in many languages, if your English is good enough. Work is likely to be on a freelance basis as needed. Contact the Institute of Translation and Interpreting to find out more about opportunities.

- Perhaps you can find a company or organisation near you that does business with your home country. They may appreciate your language skills and perhaps your knowledge of how business or other professional roles work in that country.

- Could you import a fantastic product from your home country which you know is not available here and might be demand?

- Does your home country have a particularly innovative way of approaching your field of work? Are there ways you could share that knowledge here? Perhaps you could set yourself up as a consultant.

- Remember that the whole process of moving to another country, learning a language, sorting out housing, schooling for your children, finding your way round and making new friends is a huge upheaval and uses a vast array of skills. Don't forget to point some of these out to employers. You have achieved a huge amount just to get to the point of looking for work.

Points to ponder

- You are not alone, there are millions of other people from overseas looking for work in the UK, and most of them are successful eventually.
- Make sure you understand the process of finding work here. Reading previous chapters may help!
- Ensure you are legally allowed to work in the UK.
- Make sure your English is good enough. If it is, take a test to prove it. If it isn't, take an ESOL course to improve it.
- Be prepared to take a job at a lower level in order to start on the employment ladder, at least until your English is better.
- Include experience from overseas on applications, and explain it so that an English person will understand it.
- Get an official conversion of your qualification and be prepared to do further training if necessary.
- Play to your strengths.
- Be creative about what you have to offer!

Information

UK Border Agency	www.ukba.homeoffice.gov.uk
IELTS	www.ielts.org
Next Step	nextstep.direct.gov.uk (Find a course and Job Profiles)
Private language schools	www.englishinbritain.co.uk
NARIC	www.naric.org.uk
Institute of Translation and Interpreting	www.iti.org.uk

Chapter Sixteen

Lone Parents:
Getting the Support You Need

I would like to apologise for making so many references to partners throughout this book so far. I haven't wanted to assume that everyone has a partner, but I realise the word 'partner' has come up fairly frequently. I hope you will forgive me for that!

When writing about lone parents, it is very hard to generalise, as everyone's situation is different. Some lone parents have lots of support from their children's father, who may look after the children for up to half the week, or sometimes more. Others may have no contact with their children's father at all. Whilst one lone parent may have been on their own since having children, another may have become single recently. Some lone parents rely on benefits for their main income, whilst others may be receiving differing amounts of maintenance, or have other sources of income. Many lone parents have lots of support from family and friends who live locally, whilst others have none.

What we do know is that lone parents have a hard time. They are frequently stigmatized in the media, are burdened by being the prime carer for their children and more often than not are suffering financial hardship. Recently the government changed benefits legislation, so that lone parents whose youngest child is over seven years old would have to move from Income Support to Jobseekers Allowance. In the near future this rule is likely to apply to lone parents whose youngest child is just five years old. This has meant that huge numbers of lone parents have been forced to start actively seeking work, when this had not previously been a requirement until their youngest child was sixteen.

As a lone parent, most of the issues you need to deal with in your journey back to the world of paid work will have been covered already in this book. However, there may be some other issues which you need help with. As a lone parent, seeking work is likely to be a necessity, rather than a luxury which you choose when you are ready. If you are the only one bringing an income into the family, you will need to ensure that what you earn (with top-up benefits if appropriate) is enough for your family to live on. You may also be concerned about the transition into work; will the finances add up, how will the children cope, what do I do if the children are sick?

I have no personal experience of being a lone parent, but from the many lone parents I know as friends and clients, I do know that bringing up children on your own is a mammoth task and one you should be proud of. The main advice I can give you is: don't be scared to ask for help. This chapter will concentrate on looking at the main sources of help that are out there.

Your children's father:
In their book: 'Kate and Emily's Guide to Single Parenting', Kate Ford and Emily Abbott suggest that you try to put the hurt of your break-up behind you and for the sake of your children try to forge a workable relationship with your children's father. You will always be connected in some way to him as the mother of his children, so they suggest trying to 'treat him as a business partner' in bringing up your kids together. If you can, try to gain his support for your return to work. You may need him to adjust the hours he looks after the children, help with childcare costs, be available to look after the children in emergencies and support them in any concerns they may have about new arrangements.

I realise that for many lone parents, this is all a very tall order. You may have little or no contact with your children's father, he may have died, moved to live in another part of the country, or have commitments to a new family. If you can have a conversation about it, remind him that you are 'co-parents' and that he needs to share responsibility for their care.

Family and friends
If you have family and friends locally, try to enlist their support. Talk through your plans with them, ask for ideas about the kind of work you could do, ask them to check through applications for mistakes and to be there on the end of the phone when you've had your first interview. When you start work, try to find family and friends who can be there as a backup in case of emergencies or to babysit so that you can go out and socialise with your new work colleagues.

Asking for help is not easy, but hopefully good friends will understand your situation and be willing to help. Being able to offer something back in return makes it easier for you to ask for help. You may not be able to offer to babysit in the evenings, but perhaps you could look after your friend's children on a Saturday afternoon. You could bake them a cake as a thank you, or make sure you are there to talk to when they need you. Look back at Chapter Thirteen on assertiveness and remember to ask politely but firmly for what you need and be gracious in accepting a 'no' when it is given.

Other lone parents
You are not likely to be the only lone parent in your area. There are 1.9 million single parents in the UK and 24% of all children live in a single parent family[1]. Try to find out who the lone parents are at your local toddler groups or at your children's school. Perhaps you can make friends with them and offer each other mutual support. You could use the Netmums website to contact lone parents in your area or contact Gingerbread or Onespace for information on local lone parent support groups.

Jobcentre Plus
If you are on income support or Jobseekers Allowance, you should have a Lone Parent Adviser at your Jobcentre Plus office who will be able to offer you some help:

- They may be able to do a 'better off calculation' for you to help you see how your finances would be affected by working.
- You may be able to claim an 'In Work Credit' during your first year at work, if you are working more than 16 hours per week.
- You may also be eligible for a Job Grant (currently £250) when you first start work.
- A 'Work Trial' would enable you to try out a job for three weeks, giving you and an employer a chance to try each other out – you've lost nothing if it doesn't work out.
- You may be offered training courses or help with funding a course if it helps you back to work.
- Ask about support for studying. In certain circumstances you may be able to continue claiming income support whilst studying a full or part-time course in higher education. You may also be eligible to apply for a student loan and for help with childcare expenses.

N.B. Government policy can change rapidly in this area, so the types of support offered by Jobcentre Plus may well change.

Your employer
It would be worth trying to find an employer who is likely to be sympathetic to your needs as a lone parent – look at Chapter Ten for more advice on this. You have no obligation to mention that you are a parent or indeed a lone parent when you apply for a job, but once you've started a job it may be helpful to mention your situation to

your line manager at a suitable time. It could be useful for them to know in advance that there may be occasions when have to drop everything to collect a sick child from school and that you have little back-up support. Don't forget that you have the right to time off in emergencies as explained in Chapter Eleven.

As a lone parent, who has experienced extreme challenges, I have acquired personal experience, strengths and skills which I am choosing to apply to continued self development. I experienced a high degree of isolation primarily due to the nature of my circumstances. I did not have the support of my immediate family as they were living overseas, and the majority of my friends were in partnerships.

As a woman who has experienced domestic violence, it has been fundamental to my recovery to realise I am not alone in my experience, I am capable and I am safe. As a lone parent, the repair and care of the family unit takes priority, it takes time, energy and an inexhaustible supply of commitment. I personally feel that I put myself to one side and focused absolutely on my children.

Anna

Look after yourself:
- Getting over a relationship breakdown can often take two years or more. Be gentle on yourself if you have recently become a lone parent for whatever reason.
- Being a lone parent can cause a big dent to your confidence, so look back at Chapter Three for some tips on how to boost it.
- Take it slowly, if you can. Start by doing some voluntary work and then try to work part-time, rather than making an instant move into full-time work. This will make the transition much smoother and easier to manage for both you and your children.
- On top of working, you will still have to manage caring for your children and managing everything else at home. Look at the tips in Chapter Fourteen on time management and try to get your children to help with some of the cooking, cleaning and tidying at an age-appropriate level.
- Try to make sure life isn't all work and no play. Treat yourself to a babysitter and a night out with friends once in a while, or stay in with a glass of wine and a good DVD.

Points to ponder

- If at all possible, enlist the support of your children's father. Try to see it as a business relationship.
- Swallow your pride and ask for help from friends and family. Don't be scared to be assertive and be clear about what you need.
- Meet other lone parents to share ideas and to support one another.
- Make the most of any support that's available to you.

Information

Netmums   www.netmums.com
Gingerbread   www.gingerbread.org.uk
Onespace   www.onespace.org.uk

Reading

Kate Ford & Emily Abbott, *Kate & Emily's Guide to Single Parenting,* Hay House, 2008

Rachel Morris, *The Single Parent's Handbook,* Prentice Hall Life, 2007

Chapter Seventeen

Final Thoughts

What if you're not successful?

Finding a job is not easy, it takes time, commitment, compromise and a bit of good luck! Not being successful in applications again and again can really knock your confidence. If you are struggling to find a job, review your situation and consider the following issues:

- Am I applying for the right jobs, do I have what they are looking for? Maybe you are over- or under-qualified for the jobs you are going for.
- Are you looking for work in a very competitive field? Consider broadening your search to something less popular and applying for jobs you might not have thought of before.
- Perhaps you need to update your skills and gain some more recent experience; consider doing a course or some voluntary work.
- How are your CVs and application forms? Ask a friend or careers adviser to look them over for mistakes.
- What are your interview skills like? If you are getting as far as an interview, well done you've jumped the first hurdle. If you don't then get the job, contact the employer and ask for feedback.
- It could be that you are good enough for the job, but someone else was more qualified or performed better at interview. If so, keep trying, it could be your turn next.
- Are you narrowing your options too much by only being prepared to work very specific hours? There may be very few jobs that can offer exactly what you want; you may have to compromise on something for now, whether it be pay, hours, location or type of work.

Rejection hurts; you wouldn't be human if you weren't upset by being turned down again and again. Try not to take it personally because during a time of economic downturn it's not easy to find work however skilled and experienced you are and however good your job-hunting strategy. Perhaps you need to take a couple of weeks off, review your approach and start again.

Perseverance is failing nineteen times and succeeding the twentieth.

Julie Andrews

Starting a new job – how to cope at home

If and when you are lucky enough to find a new job, congratulations! Go easy on yourself, as the change from being at home to working full or part-time and coming home to everything that still needs to be done is a big one. Starting a new job is stressful and you are bound to be exhausted by your first few days of meeting new people, trying to remember names and fitting in to a new role. The following ideas might help you to cope:

- Ask for help. Don't let your family assume that you will continue in exactly the same role as you had before. Re-read the chapter on assertiveness if you need to.
- Talk to your children about the fact that you are going back to work. Explain how things are likely to change and make sure they know how much you care about them even if you can't spend as much time together now.
- Try to be organised. Prepare packed lunches and everyone's school bags the night before, or get someone else to do it!
- Stay in touch with your friends and make time to catch up with them - you'll need their support, just as they will need yours if they go back to work.
- Make time for your children when they get home from school or childcare. Unloading the dishwasher can wait!
- Look after yourself, try to get enough sleep, eat healthily and find time for some exercise.
- Treat yourself once in a while. Use your child-free lunch break to go out for a nice coffee or a walk in the sunshine.
- Perhaps you can now afford to pay for things that save time, such as school dinners, a cleaner or an online grocery delivery – have a look at the chapter on time management for more ideas.

Starting a new job – how to cope at work

You're bound to feel nervous on your first day back at work, but it will get better. No one can hit the ground running, it takes a while to learn a new job. Consider the following tips:

- Try to avoid ringing the childminder every five minutes to find out how your child is. If they've got a problem they'll ring you.
- Leave your guilt at home, it won't achieve anything.
- Try your best to remember the names of new colleagues when you meet them. One way is to use their name when

you speak to them to reinforce the name in your mind.

- Don't be scared to ask your boss or colleagues lots of questions if you need to. No one will expect you to do your job without help on your first day.
- Try to take up opportunities to socialise with your colleagues if you can. It's a good way of getting to know people and starting to feel part of the team.
- Before children you may have stayed in the office till late at night to finish off something for a deadline. That may not be possible any more. How will you deal with that? Could your partner or a friend pick up the children from nursery if you have a deadline? Perhaps you could take something home to finish off in the evening or maybe you need to stop being such a perfectionist. How about talking to your boss about your workload, or ask for more warning of a deadline?
- You may find it helpful to talk to your employer about the fact that you have children and that you will need to leave promptly at the end of the day. Make it clear that this does not diminish your commitment to your job, but that you will work hard to get your job done in the hours that you are there. Ensuring that they know you have children will mean that it is not such a shock to them when you have to take the day off because your child is sick.

Finally, good luck as you start out on what I hope will be an exciting new journey for you. I hope that you enjoy your new career and continue to enjoy your family.

Cambridge Women's Resources Centre

Cambridge Women's Resources Centre (CWRC) opened in 1982 to provide women with quality vocational training, support, guidance and recreational activities in a women only environment.

CWRC provides vocational training in Computing and pre-vocational training in English, Maths and ESOL (English for Speakers of Other Languages). These courses are accredited and lead to nationally recognised qualifications. We also offer a range of courses to increase personal resources such as Return to Work, Personal Safety & Self Defence.

We have an on-site crèche available to all women using the centre's facilities. We also have vocational guidance available to women using the centre. In addition, the centre provides a number of drop-in facilities including internet access.

www.cwrc.org.uk

Bekki Clark can be contacted at bekkiclark@hotmail.co.uk

References for each chapter:

Chapter One:
[1] www.abravenewworld.co.uk/articles/2007/08/html
[2] 3.4 million women with dependent children (0-18), not in paid work in the second quarter of 2008, according to the Labour Force Survey Q2 2008
[3] The Women and Work Commission, *Shaping a Fairer Future* 2007 (from the 2005 Labour Force Survey)
[4] Office for National Statistics: *Work and Family Report* 02/12/09 Figures for the second quarter of 2008 http://www.statistics.gov.uk/cci/nugget.asp?id=1655

Chapter Three:
[1.] Haygroup; *Women's Work Report* (2006)
[2.] Susan Jeffers, *Feel The Fear and Do It Anyway,* Vermillion, 2007

Chapter Four:
[1] www.liberateyourtalent.com, *Maximising your potential in the changing world of work*, 2010
[2] www.business.timesonline.co.uk (Best 100 Companies)
[3, 4] ONS, *Women in the Labour Market* March 09
[5] ONS, *Working Lives* Sep 08
[6] Vera Baird, *Women Need Better Part-Time Work,* www.equalities.gov.uk Feb 10
[7] The Women and Work Commission, *Shaping a fairer future,* 2006
[8] http://www.part-time-jobs-london.co.uk/top-5-recession-proof-jobs Jan 2010

Chapter Six:
[1] Hay Group, *Women's Work* (2006). www.haygroup.co.uk

Chapter Seven:
[1] *Could 'Achievement Amnesia' Cost You Your Career? Contrasting what employers want from CVs, with what Jobseekers give them.* Research report by www.iprofile.org, 2008
[2] Farhan Yasin, *What Employers Want to See on Your CV,* www.careerbuilder.co.uk Sep 09

Chapter Nine:
[1] Equality and Human Rights Commission www.equalityhumanrights.com

Chapter Ten:
[1] *The Great Work Debate.* www.netmums.com (2005)
[2] Adapted from "Flexible Working Factsheet" www.workingfamilies.org.uk 2008

Chapter Thirteen:
[1] Thomas A. Harris, *I'm OK, You're OK,* Arrow Books Ltd, 1995
[2] Liz Willis & Jenny Daisley, *Springboard Women's Development Workbook,* Hawthorn Press, 2008

Chapter Fifteen:
[1] 534,000 people arrived in the UK in the year to March 2009: Office for National Statistics *Migration Statistics Quarterly Report,* No 3 November 2009

Chapter Sixteen
[1] www.gingerbread.org.uk 'Single parent statistics'